HUNDRED MILE
PRAYER WALK

Around Lancashire

D0272978

HUNDRED MILE PRAYER WALK

AROUND LANCASHIRE

Rev. Canon Herrick Daniel

Sovereign World

LANCASTER COUNTY LIBRARY

3011812075637 8	
HJ	27-Jan-2011
248.32 HER	£8.99

Published by Sovereign World Ltd
PO Box 784
Ellel
Lancaster
LA1 9DA
United Kingdom

www.sovereignworld.com

Copyright © 2010 Herrick Daniel.

All rights reserved. No part of this publication may be reproduced, stored in a retrieval system, or transmitted in any form or by any means, electronic, mechanical, photocopying or otherwise, without the prior written consent of the publisher. Short extracts may be used for review purposes.

Unless otherwise stated, all Scripture quotations are taken from the New Revised Standard Version. Copyright © 1989 by the Division of Christian Education of the National Council of the Churches of Christ in the USA.

Other versions used are:

RSV – Revised Standard Version. Copyright © 1946, 1952, 1971 (the Apocrypha is copyrighted 1957, 1977) by the Division of Christian Education of the National Council of the Churches of Christ in the USA.

NIV – Scripture quotations marked (NIV) are taken from the Holy Bible, New International Version®, NIV®. Copyright © 1973, 1978, 1984 by Biblica, Inc.™ Used by permission of Zondervan. All rights reserved worldwide.

NKJV – Scripture quotations marked "NKJV™" are taken from the New King James Version®. Copyright © 1982 by Thomas Nelson, Inc. Used by permission. All rights reserved.

KJV – Scripture quotations marked "KJV" are taken from the Holy Bible, King James Version, Cambridge, 1769.

NLT – Scripture quotations marked NLT are taken from the Holy Bible, New Living Translation, copyright © 1996, 2004. Used by permission of Tyndale House Publishers, Inc., Wheaton, Illinois 60189. All rights reserved.

GNB – Scriptures and additional materials quoted are from the Good News Bible © 1994 published by the Bible Societies/HarperCollins Publishers Ltd UK, Good News Bible © American Bible Society 1966, 1971, 1976, 1992. Used with permission.

The Servant Song /Richard Gillard Copyright ©1977 Scripture In Song (a div. of Integrity Music, Inc.)/ASCAP All rights reserved. Used by permission.

ISBN: 978-1-85240-541-0

The publishers aim to produce books which will help to extend and build up the Kingdom of God. We do not necessarily agree with every view expressed by the authors, or with every interpretation of Scripture expressed. We expect readers to make their own judgment in the light of their understanding of God's Word and in an attitude of Christian love and fellowship.

Cover design by ThirteenFour Design
Cover images courtesy of the Lancashire Evening Telegraph
Typeset by Hurix
Printed in the United Kingdom

CONTENTS

ACKNOWLEDGEMENTS

I am especially indebted to my two precious colleagues, Bishop Geoff Pearson and Reverend Sam Corley, with whom I shared in prayer, friendship and fellowship during the eight days' prayer walk.

Grateful thanks to the churches and hundreds of people who supported us, fed and looked after us so well during our visit to their churches and communities. Their fellowship, prayer, guidance, help, information, advice and, in some cases, accompanying us on the walk, have had an invaluable impact on this book.

My special thanks to Mrs Anne Mansley, Rachel Daniel, Hannah Daniel and Naomi Daniel for typing the manuscript, which no doubt many people will be benefiting from their laborious work. The manuscript has also been vastly improved by amendments suggested by my wife, Judy Daniel who also read it and made corrections where necessary. Reviewing a book can be a painful process, which is why I am grateful to Reverend Bob Street for undertaking this daunting task for me. Many thanks to the Bishop of Blackburn, Rt Reverend Nicholas Reade for his contribution in writing the foreword for my book.

Writing a book of this kind is not easy to get all the information 100% correct, therefore I apologise to any church where I may have made any error in the information recorded. Thanking you in anticipation of favourable consideration.

Extra care has been taken to do justice to all the churches visited and hope very much that the information presented in this book will be a source of encouragement to them and will benefit others richly.

It has been said that no two flowers are the same, although in appearances some of them may look alike. Similarly in the contents of the book, particularly from day one to day eight it may appear as if I am repeating myself, especially where hospitality is concerned. If occurred then the repetition is deliberate. The reason is because all the churches visited made special efforts to make elaborate feasts for us, therefore, it is an appropriate way of acknowledging their generosities, so that when they read the book they will see that their special effort has not been summarised into one paragraph at the end in culmination of bundling everybody together to say thank you all.

I would also like to thank the team at Sovereign World for the publishing of this book, especially to Paul Stanier for his advice and assistance.

Above all, I thank and praise God to whom this book is dedicated to His glory, for sustaining, providing and giving us enough strength to complete the eight days' prayer walk satisfactorily.

I am pleased to issue some questions at the back of the book for discussion. Feel free to duplicate them as much as necessary.

FOREWORD

You will find in these pages some interesting facts and historical accounts, and we are frequently brought back to the Word of God. Herrick's writings show us something of the spiritual life of a priest who has had a long and busy ministry but also found time to stop, look and listen, and that listening and looking is prayer.

This book will help us to "feel the gentle breeze of the Spirit". May we too, on our longer journey through life, find that time to stop, listen and look. I assure you this is a good read and you will find here the thoughts and reflections of one pilgrim which will help us on our journey as we climb to the top of the mountain to the full vision of God.

The Bishop of Blackburn, The Rt Revd Nicholas Reade

Official logo duplicated with kind permission of the
Prayer Walk Organiser: Reverend Sam Corley.

INTRODUCTION

In recent years prayer walking has become increasingly popular, as many Christians are discovering more and more that prayer is a practical activity. When the March for Jesus took to the streets about twenty years ago, a large number of churches quickly discovered and experienced in reality a refreshing upsurge of creativity in praising and worshipping God, above all to communicate with Him through prayer, music, inspiring words, drama, art, liturgical dance, and with display of flags and banners. Also, enthusiastic Christians rediscovered a new and fresh vision of praying, while pounding the street, to share God's love and truth in a demonstrative way.

It was this inspiring vision of prayer that captivated my heart and mind to join with two other colleagues, Reverend Sam Corley and Bishop Geoff Pearson, to embark upon a prayer walk journey around the diocese of Blackburn in Lancashire. We set off on 24 May 2009 and completed our journey on 31 May, covering approximately 109 miles walk in eight days. During that time we visited forty-four churches and prayed inside forty-three of them, as well as praying outside other churches (some of them were sadly closed), and in various institutions, including schools, clubs and other organisations, as well as for individuals.

It was an incredible journey of prayer, faith, determination, strength, excitement, persistency, joy and hard work, when we were duly tested in many areas – not to mention the weather!

The book is factual and inspirational, yet it is written with humour and cheerfulness, and includes a wide range of colourful characteristics of landscape, hidden corners of villages, town history, and descriptions of churches and ministry as a whole. The detail, drama, excitement, important information, and the powerful drive within that kept us going, and the parish life and ministry of the churches visited will be revealed.

It is my prayer that this memorable journey will not only open a fresh window into the minds of all those who are dutifully concerned about successful ministry in their beloved diocese, but will also open a new window of optimistic hope into the minds of all readers searching and wishing to embrace a powerful life of prayer, victorious Christian life, courage in the face of danger, strength in times of weakness, stimulation in times of dryness, power to conquer fear, restoration of remnant ministry, and potential hope for the future.

Reverend Canon Herrick Daniel, summer 2010

Chapter 1

MY CALL TO THE PRAYER WALK

People are called to vocational ministry in different ways and through various circumstances, and prayer ministry is one such vocation with special consideration of a divine calling. I wish therefore to explain how the call came to me to join two other clergymen in praying around the diocese of Blackburn.

One bright Sunday in January 2009, my wife Judy and I went to a morning service at the parish church of St John the Evangelist, Ellel, Lancaster, and came back to our house with a one-page notice sheet. While sitting in the comfort of our living room, Judy observed in the sheet some information about a prayer walk around the diocese. Knowing my keen interest in prayer, she immediately drew my attention to the paragraph on the prayer walk, with its reference to Reverend Sam Corley and Bishop Geoff Pearson giving an open invitation to anyone interested in joining the duo.

Judy and I discussed the prospect of this prayer venture, and I decided to follow it up, which led to a telephone call to Geoff, who agreed to meet me at his office on Monday 26 January at 2.00 pm. My interest was subsequently conveyed to Sam, who was pleased with the thought of having me on the prayer walk with them. Eventually Sam and I talked about it at great length and concluded that I would think about the commitment it would incur. This was the point that I searchingly brought my intention before God's throne of grace in prayer.

Part of the answer came through Sam's announcement to the congregation at St Paul's Church, Scotforth, where we were attending a united Lent course on – guess what? – 'Prayer'! Sam, in consultation with the senior diocesan staff, had been given the sole responsibility of visiting all six deaneries where the Lent prayer course was being held in various churches to encourage more people to join the prayer walk.

A desire emerged in me during this service on the theme of prayer, especially with the challenging announcement from Sam to pray further for definite confirmation from the Lord, especially with the realisation that this was a big commitment involving dedication, lots of prayer, training, fitness, time and long distance walking to cover over 100 miles. I wanted to be absolutely certain that God wanted me to take part in this great venture.

As well as praying about it, I took many other things into consideration. Firstly, I asked myself several questions I felt I should have put to Sam: 'What is the object of this prayer exercise? What are we hoping to achieve at the end of it all? What kind of response are we hoping to get from church officials?' Having missed the opportunity to ask Sam these vital questions, I satisfied myself with answers I believed were reasonable.

I took a long look at the conditions of most churches in the diocese and came to the conclusion that they were desperately in need of prayer. It was very clear to me that they would benefit from a spiritual revolution which I believed would be brought about through persistent prayer. Secondly, I thought that both the clergy and lay workers of the churches needed support, and that our presence with them would reassure them, and would demonstrate how much we cared for them in their difficult ministry. Thirdly, they would hopefully see it as an official diocesan gesture of love, concern and support. Furthermore, I concluded that the intrinsic value of prayer in itself was indispensable and, as such, it was something that I would enjoy doing, taking into consideration its importance.

With the green light flashing to go ahead, the next step was to ask Sam some practical questions; this time about the journey itself, such as where would we be sleeping during the eight days walking around? The answer given was that we would sleep at our homes when it was convenient, and the rest of the time in various homes around the diocese. Secondly, what would we do about food during that time? I was told that a main meal would be provided by churches at key points in the diocese, and that we would carry sandwiches for in between main meals. The reasons given were that if we spent too much time eating proper meals in too many churches, we couldn't complete the 100 miles in the time specified; which made sense.

A crucial question put to Sam was, what would we do for toilet facilities on the way? I was assured that if we wore our clerical collars, the pubs on the route would surely let us use their lavatories! Even more urgent was the question of how we would carry all our equipment and other necessities. A welcome answer, which pleased my ears, was that a minibus would follow us to carry our heavy equipment, including sleeping bags and so on. As it turned out, the man who had agreed to drive the minibus sadly fell ill a few weeks before the walk, so alternative arrangements had to be made accordingly.

Other questions were raised, such as the possibility of heavy rain during the walk, or how we could walk safely along potentially dangerous busy roads. We agreed that we would cross these bridges when we came to them. However, if it was virtually impossible to walk in certain areas, we would have no choice but to ride in the minibus.

Chapter 2

THE PREPARATION

Preparation for any important event is vital to achieve one's goal successfully. This is a lesson that every athlete learns before running a race; in preparing for the race, certain rules of discipline must be observed, such as going to bed at the right time, having the right kind of food and drink, and working hard in training. An ideal example is given by David Wilkie, the British gold medallist in Montreal in 1976, who made reference on his return to Britain how he had worked hard to achieve a great reward.

Similarly, a few months leading to the long prayer walk, I was training very hard for the occasion. I went to the gym regularly for my usual workout, followed by swimming and steam bath sessions. I also kept up with my regular running, which I enjoy doing anyway, as well as going for long walks to prepare for what was to come. I remember vividly going to the gym for adequate training, involving a good workout every single day in the week before the walk actually started. I was trying at the same time not to overwork myself so that I did not get tired shortly before the big day. People who are not used to gym exercises may be tempted to ask the question, 'Was the effort worth it?' or 'Was it sensible to visit the gym the whole week before such a long walk?' The short answer to this question would be simply 'Yes', but to elaborate: It is interesting that I have found from my own experience that when I spend a good session or a good week in the gym I usually feel much fitter than before. So I satisfied myself with the thought that every pound of weight that I pumped in the air during the last week before the walk was worth it.

The apostle Paul compared the Christian life training to running a race. In fact, it is stated in Hebrews, 'let us run with perseverance the race that is set before us, looking to Jesus the pioneer and perfecter of our faith, who for the sake of the joy that was set before him endured the cross, disregarding its shame, and has taken his seat at the right hand of the throne of God' (Hebrews 12:1,2, NRSV). The apostle now talks in gymnastic style when he says: 'Everyone who competes in the games goes into strict training. They do it to get a crown that will not last; but we do it to get a crown that will last forever. Therefore I do not run like a man running aimlessly; I do not fight like a man beating the air. No I beat my body and make it my slave so that after I have preached to others, I myself will not be disqualified for the prize' (1 Corinthians 9:25–27, NIV).

A few days before the walk actually started, I searched through several shoe shops for something suitable to wear, and I eventually bought two pairs of trainers from a market in Lancaster, which felt comfortable. Other necessities were carefully considered, such as suitable clothes, medicine, food, money and so on. Meanwhile, Sam was engaged in preparing the route and map detail which has been regarded as the companion of every traveller. Not an easy task, especially with the diocese of Blackburn's large geographical areas stretching from Silverdale to Blackpool, and covering an area of 878 square miles.

In addition, Sam had written letters to all the ministers and other representatives in the diocese that we were planning to visit on the way, explaining the purpose and the day and time that we would be visiting their church in particular. A few days before we set off most of the representatives had thankfully replied to the request signifying a 'yes' agreement, with only a few pending. However, we lived in expectation that by the time we set off on the journey all, or at least 99 per cent, would have replied satisfactorily, which turned out to be the case.

Having satisfied ourselves that we were as ready as we could possibly be, taking into consideration the busy life of a clergyman, we finally decided that this was the end of phase one and were now preparing for phase two. Sam made arrangements to pick up the minibus on the morning of the walk, between the hours of 6.00 and 7.00 am from a distance of approximately three to four miles away. It was one of those circumstances that were inevitable, because the alternative was to keep the bus outside Sam's house the day before but, unfortunately, because it was hired, this meant that the extra day would have made a big difference in terms of cost. Therefore, it was organised to be picked up on the same day to avoid unnecessary expense, which was a wise decision at this time of economic recession.

At this point, when the inevitability of the day arrived with just hours before stepping outside the door, my feelings seemed to heighten with mixed emotion that prompted the question: Is it God's will to do this great venture? The answer seemed to come in my daily Bible reading. To my amazement the psalm for the morning before setting off was Psalm 116 – it was so relevant to the journey.

> I love the LORD, because he has heard
>   my voice and my supplications.
> Because he inclined his ear to me,
>   therefore I will call on him as long as I live.
> The snares of death encompassed me;
>   the pangs of Sheol laid hold on me;
>   I suffered distress and anguish.
> Then I called on the name of the LORD:
>   'O LORD, I pray, save my life!'
>
> Gracious is the LORD, and righteous;
>   our God is merciful.
> The LORD protects the simple;
>   when I was brought low, he saved me.
> Return, O my soul, to your rest,
>   for the LORD has dealt bountifully with you.
>
> For you have delivered my soul from death,
>   my eyes from tears,
>   my feet from stumbling.
> I walk before the LORD
>   in the land of the living.
> I kept my faith, even when I said,
>   'I am greatly afflicted';
> I said in my consternation,
>   'Everyone is a liar.'
>
> What shall I return to the LORD
>   for all his bounty to me?

I will lift up the cup of salvation
and call on the name of the LORD,
I will pay my vows to the LORD
in the presence of all his people.
Precious in the sight of the LORD
is the death of his faithful ones.
O LORD, I am your servant;
I am your servant, the child of your serving-maid.
You have loosed my bonds.
I will offer to you a thanksgiving sacrifice
and call on the name of the LORD.
I will pay my vows to the LORD
in the presence of all his people,
in the courts of the house of the LORD,
in your midst, O Jerusalem.
Praise the LORD!
(NRSV)

There are three elements that caught my attention. Again and again the appeal is made in calling upon the Lord in various circumstances. Secondly, verse 8 states, 'For you have delivered my soul from death, my eyes from tears, my *feet* from stumbling' (my italics). Thirdly, verse 9 says, 'I walk before the LORD in the land of the living.' One could imagine when I saw the words 'feet' and 'walk' in a positive context the very morning literally a few minutes before setting off, it was extremely reassuring that I was doing the right thing. In fact, this gave me the green light to go because God was with me. It boosted my confidence and increased my faith considerably. Even more surprising, the next verse says: 'I kept my faith'. I said to myself that this was far too much to be a coincidence. With this in mind, my strength and energy levels seemed to rise up like an eagle and made me ready for the road with no hesitation.

When I came back in the evening, approximately 9.00 pm, my reading before retiring to my bed was Psalm 119:1–8. Again, it's worth recording this Bible passage here to see how reassuring it was to me after completing the day satisfactorily:

Blessed are those whose way is blameless,
who walk in the law of the LORD!
Blessed are those who keep his testimonies,

who seek him with their whole heart,
who also do no wrong,
but walk in his ways!
Thou hast commanded thy precepts
to be kept diligently.
O that my ways may be steadfast
in keeping thy statutes!
Then I shall not be put to shame,
having my eyes fixed on all thy commandments.
I will praise thee with an upright heart,
when I learn thy righteous ordinances.
I will observe thy statutes;
O forsake me not utterly!
(RSV)

Once more, three elements are striking in this evening passage of the first day. Firstly, praising God in verse 7 and blessing which is mentioned in verses 1 and 2. Secondly, the word 'walk' is miraculously mentioned twice in this short passage; again, verses 1 and 2. Also, the word 'ways' is mentioned twice as well, in verses 3 and 5. Matthew Henry, the great seventeenth-century preacher and expositioner, with his spiritual insight maintained that the psalmist shows in these verses that godly people are happy people who make the will of God the rule in all their actions, that they walk in the paths of God's Word, and they walk in God's ways (vv. 1,3). Of course, it is an honour of the highest obligation to walk in God's way and in accordance with His will.

Chapter 3

PRAYING AROUND:
REVEREND SAM CORLEY

I first had the idea for a prayer walk around the diocese when I was appointed Assistant Missioner in January 2008. I had come to the diocese four years previously to be curate of St Thomas' Lancaster, so there were still many places in the diocese that I had heard much about, but had never visited – I was keen to explore!

Initially I set about driving around some of the major towns and cities to get more of a feel for places and to see how close they were to each other. At the time I was well aware that such an exercise can only give one a very superficial introduction to a place; but it was at least a start.

Over the weeks that followed, I considered how to develop this initial understanding, and the idea of praying whilst walking around the diocese emerged. At first I planned to do this quietly by myself, but the Lord spoke clearly to me about inviting others to join with me in this pilgrimage of prayer. A good part of the reason for this, I believe, was as a way of encouraging the whole diocese to focus on praying for its mission and ministry for a set period. After a brief conversation with Bishop Nicholas Reade it seemed sensible to do this in the period between Ascension Day and Pentecost Sunday – a novena, or nine days, of prayer seeking the Lord's presence, blessing and power during this holy season.

I was thrilled to have the support of Bishop Geoff from a very early stage, and was delighted when he was the first to agree to walk with me. Others quickly offered to walk with us for parts of the adventure, and Bishop Geoff and I were both pleased when Herrick Daniel asked if he might get involved for the whole walk after hearing the Lord call him to join us.

So began the process of planning the walk and deciding on which churches to visit as we moved in an anticlockwise direction around the diocese – beginning in Silverdale and ending in Fleetwood.

Throughout the walk we were moved by the warmth of those who received us, the seriousness with which people joined with us in praying for their local church and community, and by the enthusiasm for the walk to be repeated. As I write, plans are already well underway for a second walk that will follow a different route in 2010.

Chapter 4

SENSE OF ADVENTURE:
BISHOP GEOFF PEARSON

A prayer walk around the Blackburn diocese had significant appeal for me. As someone interested in the Celtic Church, I felt here was a chance for adventure. For the most part, a bishop in the modern Church is a servant of the institution. You are running, it feels, to keep the institution going, and there are too few opportunities to venture into new things for Christ.

The Roman pattern of parishes and dioceses may well be the most suitable for settled communities and a commonly accepted faith, but we are increasingly facing a non-Christian or semi-Christian situation. As early as the sixth century, individuals in the Celtic Church set out to spread the faith because they were excited by the gospel. The prayer adventure around the diocese was not quite in the steps of the 'peregrinati' (wanderers) who often set off for faraway places not knowing if they would ever return. Nor was it like the bishop in the early Celtic communities who was subordinate to the abbot in the monastery but who went out in evangelistic mission, often with a small team.

But yes, there was a mission sense about this adventure around the diocese. Although for the most part operating within the safety of the Church across the diocese, nevertheless we would be praying, we would be open to Holy Spirit surprises, and we would be trusting God for His provision.

As I reflect on our pilgrimage around the diocese, I remember with thanksgiving many aspects of our walk. Being part of a small, intimate group of three that walked, prayed and lived together for the most part was a real blessing. Bishoping can be a lonely role, and the friendship of colleagues on the walk was a bonus I had not anticipated.

Then there was a bigger circle of people we met along the way. Some we knew already and some were new people who came into our lives. I came back, like the proverbial shepherd, with a deeper knowledge of the sheep and new insights into the mission and ministry of many of our churches.

In my head, I am aware of God's loving provision. I, like many Christians have examples of how God has provided in the past. But it is so easy to stay in the comfort zone and live off past experiences. Here was a chance to prove God and experience a bit more living by faith than the normal week at Shireshead Vicarage. I have been on previous missions under the banner of a 'Walk of a Thousand Men', and have always returned with faith levels higher and an excitement about God at work in people's lives. And the walk in May 2009 was no exception. Whether it was food or guides with local knowledge or strategic lifts or whatever, there was more than adequate provision.

In this book, Herrick Daniel has given his overview of the walk. He has recalled just some of the many encounters along the walking route. His context of many of the churches and places we visited is most illuminating. But a bit like the Gospels, I was on the same walk yet recall some different encounters. Not everything, I realise, could be included. Not even the sick people I prayed with or the 'For Sale' signs in so many business outlets. But, having encountered so much that was positive in our churches, it was a reminder at the end of the walk on Pentecost Sunday how much we need to go on being filled with the Holy Spirit. For a short period the walkers moved from the safe and the predictable to the unusual and the charismatic. There was a certain spontaneity about each day and that does wonders for the prayer life. It was an experiment that some of us are anxious to repeat.

Chapter 5

DAY ONE
SUNDAY 24 MAY

Silverdale

Carnforth

Bolton-Le-Sands

Slyne with Hest

Morecambe

Lancaster

Ready Steady Go

On 24 May 2009, as the clock in our living room was fast approaching 7.00 am, I was anxiously waiting for the doorbell to ring. Then, under the blue sky on that bright sunny day, the minibus arrived. Sam greeted me with a smile which seemed to say that there was no going back, therefore there was only one way open to us and that was forward. In writing my notes, I couldn't help but think of the popular song 'Here we go.' Sam was eager to give me a helping hand with my suitcase, and I carried my other bag to the bus.

As the bus slowly moved off and picked up more speed down the hill, my house and street gradually disappeared on the horizon. We were going to pick up Bishop Geoff at Shireshead, a distance of about three miles away. The short drive occupied Sam and me in conversation about the expectation of the walk and the need to be flexible. Soon the bus slowly pulled in to a car park next to the bishop's house, and within minutes Geoff arrived with his case, bishop's crook in his hand and wearing shorts. He greeted us with a broad smile and commented that he was suitably dressed for the weather and that his faith had compelled him to put on his shorts because he sincerely believed that the sun would shine for the day. Some people would say from their experience one can never trust the English weather, as it is quite possible to get all four seasons in one day. It was therefore necessary to ask, was it an act of faith or an act of folly? I am pleased to say that he was right. The good Lord was very gracious to us and caused the sun to shine all day, which proved it to be an act of faith.

It was a pleasant journey between Lancaster and Silverdale – which took approximately twenty-five minutes on the winding road – especially as this time in the morning the road was rather quiet.

Our first stop was at St John's Silverdale where the incumbent, Canon Paul Warren, cheerfully met and greeted us with a smile in front of the sleepy church. After a brief chat about the journey and the prospect of the long day ahead of us, he informally commissioned us and, after praying for God's guidance, protection, provision and presence with us, he gave the blessing and bid us well on our way. We thanked him most sincerely and set off happily from Silverdale on our long walk to Carnforth, with our rucksacks strapped tightly on our backs.

When one sets off on an ambitious expedition, one of the first requirements is the use of a map to locate position and where one is on the route. This was readily available in Sam's hands. He held it shoulder high and indicated to us the precise point of departure and where we would be travelling next. With Geoff and I unanimously in agreement we set off in the direction indicated on the map, to discover a few minutes later that we had taken the wrong turning. This mistake was quickly rectified in good humour, with the hope that this wouldn't become a regular pattern during our epic walk.

Following a short discussion with regard to the options open to us, we decided to walk across the marsh, which we anticipated would be relatively more difficult but quicker than the longer distance on the main road. Fortunately, we had a local walker, Anne Wittington, who was accompanying us from the start at St John's, Emesgate Lane in Silverdale. She came as a result of notification which had been given to churches in the diocese about the prayer journey. Anne, who had her dog with her, accompanied us for about fifteen minutes and then had to return back because of other commitments. She thoroughly enjoyed it and we were glad to have her chatting to us about the church and the environmental condition of the area.

Walking across the marsh for the first time on a bright sunny day was for me an unforgettable experience. The magical scenery of the marsh and some glittering streams below a bridge we crossed, and witnessing grass waving gently in the warm breeze was something of near-perfect beauty. There were few other places in the whole of the diocese during the course of the walk that offered such majestic views with such airy cliffs, and colourful meadows and fields under the clear blue sky.

Although, on occasions, we were forced to pass through some muddy fields, rough footpaths, steep hills, undulating tracks and narrow gates, all these did not outweigh the sheer beauty of the open countryside. In fact, I was reminded of Matthew 7:14 where Jesus says, 'the gate is narrow and the way is hard, that leads to life, and those who find it are few' (RSV). Interestingly, we had to look very hard before we found the narrow gate to take us across the marsh, because it was not clearly marked, which made this inspirational text even more significant for our walk with the Lord.

When we eventually arrived at the top of a steep hill, I couldn't resist stopping to take some photographs with my digital camera of the magnificent view down below, looking right across Morecambe Bay, which is famous for its many attractions. On setting off from there, I observed the occasional birds soaring around while making their varied calls.

The combination of the rolling countryside, the inspirational bird-song, the breathtaking view, the running water of streams, the magnificent landscape, the green trees and the lovely sunshine projecting warmth from above, made me aware of God's infinite power to create and maintain all these things. This explains fully why the psalmist says: 'The earth is the LORD's, and everything in it, the world, and all who live in it; for he founded it upon the seas and established it upon the waters' (Psalm 24:1,2, NIV). Admiring the beauty of God's creation, as we walked and prayed, was something special.

Suddenly Sam's mobile rang. It was a call from Joe Wilson from Radio Lancashire, who was enquiring about the walk and our

position. Sam, who had made prior arrangements to communicate with the radio presenter during the walk, chatted to him for
about ten minutes, with Geoff sealing the conversation with his
approval. The conversation with Joe Wilson went out live on the
Sunday morning radio programme, which was the main object of
the call.

Was the interruption from the prayer walking session justified?
This is a good question one may be tempted to ask. It may be true
to say that Radio Lancashire has a wide range of listeners and, as
a result of the live communication, it was an ideal opportunity
for the listeners to be informed of what was happening on the
prayer walk and to explain the value of prayer and intercession
as such.

Intercession is the crowning ministry of the Christian life and
certainly a powerful force in the church sector, as manifested by the
Spirit. The apostle Paul captures the spirit of an indwelling intercessor
when he writes: 'Likewise the Spirit also helps in our weaknesses.
For we do not know what we should pray for as we ought, but
the Spirit Himself makes intercession for us with groanings which
cannot be uttered. Now He who searches the hearts knows what the
mind of the Spirit is, because He makes intercession for the saints
according to the will of God' (Romans 8:26,27, NKJV).

Becoming an intercessor on a long prayer walk journey of eight
days is not easy because it cuts into our time, makes exceptional demands upon our energy, persistently tests our patience and, above
all, forces us to rearrange our priorities.

Some may ask the question why we decided to walk over 100
miles in the diocese of Blackburn to visit so many churches? My
answer is, simply to demonstrate our love, care and concern for
churches in the diocese and to show it in practical ways in praying
with them; also, to listen to their problems, needs and concerns and
to give them advice accordingly. This means to stand with them in
their time of need.

On our epic journey we discovered that the demand for intercession in the churches visited was so great that comparatively few true
dedicated intercessors were involved in it. The kind of intercession I
am talking about here requires much more than a few minutes on a
Sunday morning/evening, or adding to the midweek Bible study, or
praying for friends and loved ones.

It has been said that a true intercessor will observe what has been called the three laws. Firstly, to focus one's total attention upon the greatness of God, especially upon His mighty power, omnipotence and accessibility through the living Jesus Christ. Secondly, to dedicate oneself to God fully and to decide properly how much time one is able to give daily or weekly in prayer. Thirdly, to ask God sincerely to lay the needs upon one's heart of what to pray for.

The journey between St John's Church in Silverdale and Christ Church in Carnforth covers a distance of about six and a half miles. Having arrived at Christ Church at 11.00 am, by the grace of God, we were warmly greeted by the incumbent, Reverend Stephen Jones.

This is the point that Sam had to return to Silverdale to pick up the minibus as previously agreed. Luckily he was able to catch the train, which happened to depart near to the time we arrived on that particular station, which was pleasing to all of us as we were particularly keen to keep to our time schedule.

Geoff and I were given strict instructions by Sam to wait around until he returned, which we gladly accepted. The thought of waiting for Sam for about an hour or so came as a welcome relief after our long walk across the marsh. After Sam hurried down the platform to catch the train, Geoff and I decided to walk around the area until he returned. First of all we went up the little hill leading to the biggest second-hand bookshop in Lancashire, with a stock of books in the region of 100,000, but because it happened to be a Sunday morning, it was closed. We then followed Plan B which was to move around the supermarket car park area with high expectations of carrying out friendship evangelism to the shoppers, but the catch on this occasion was rather poor. However, we did manage to smile and have short conversations with a few people who seemed to have one dominating factor on their minds – shopping.

Sam managed to drive safely to Slyne and rejoined us on his bicycle. We prayed for the various needs of Christ Church in Carnforth and the community as a whole, which were presented to us by the church officials, and walked to Bolton-le-Sands where we arrived at approximately 1.00 pm. Having received a warm and hearty welcome from a warden called Kathleen, we quickly discovered that it was time to eat our lunch from our bags, with a drink generously given by the church workers. We happened to arrive at the same time a baptism was taking place inside the church. With our tummies crying out for food, we responded by having our lunch in the cemetery, sitting on whatever we could find that supported the weight of our tired bodies!

The local newspaper's photographer (who seemed to have no regard for our crying tummies) was in a hurry to line us up on the top of a wall adjacent to the church, facing the main road. He hurriedly took a few pictures of us, accompanied by the church members who were present, to support the newspaper's story of the walk, and quickly moved on to his next project.

The photographic session outside and the baptism service inside the church finished simultaneously, so without wasting any more time we all agreed to occupy the church building immediately for a time of extemporary prayer with church officials who supplied us with various needs to pray about.

Having completed our prayer session, we made our way to Slyne, arriving there just before 3.00 pm, where the incumbent, Reverend Pauline Bicknell, and other church officials joyfully welcomed us at St Luke's Church. The weather was sunny and inviting so we all agreed to sit around a table outside to be fed with plenty of information about the church's needs, which kept us occupied in intercessory prayer for nearly thirty minutes. The parishioners fed us to the brim before departing.

Canal walk

One of the distinctive characteristics of our journey so far was the ideal opportunity to walk alongside the canal, which we all thoroughly enjoyed. Some parishioners from the previous church joined us, which was quite rewarding as they were able to share their stories with us while walking along.

The canal has a long history that goes right back to the eighteenth century and has been compared to our modern motorway in carrying bulky cargoes such as coal, limestone, grain and other goods. It has also been popular for recreational purposes such as fishing, canoeing, swimming, pleasure boats and, in winter, skating and other leisure activities.

On the way we saw some people were parading their dogs. They occasionally greeted us with smiling faces. Of course, over the years the beauty of canal walks has inspired many walkers.

Unfortunately, circumstances compelled us to use the minibus to Morecambe. We arrived at 4.00 pm and some of the church members were already there, patiently waiting for us at Holy Trinity Church, despite the fact that they were going through an interregnum at the time of our visit. (An 'interregnum' means the period of time between the minister leaving a church and the appointment of the new minister taking over.) After some refreshments kindly provided by the parishioners, we were duly informed of ten items for prayer which we heartily welcomed and, having been joined by the group present, we prayed for them accordingly.

Our visit to Morecambe gave us the golden opportunity to see the town that has been described as 'the lungs' of Lancashire. Morecambe's large beaches and wide bay have attracted visitors from all over Britain. It has maintained a famous reputation from the beginning of the twentieth century for its varied entertainment such as funfairs, amusement arcades and theatres. Overlooking the seafront and Marineland on the stone jetty was what was claimed to be Europe's first oceanarium, which had a well-stocked aquarium and performing dolphins. However, in recent years it has become sadly rundown, compared to the time when the illumination lights were second only to Blackpool, drawing large crowds from all over.

Morecambe's famous walk across the bay at low tide from Hesketh Bank to Grange over Sands is a popular venture for keen walkers. The distance is approximately eight miles, and walkers are accompanied by an official guide who has an extensive knowledge of the safe route to follow. Among other attractions in Morecambe is the famous statue of the late comedian Eric Morecambe, which attracts a stream of visitors, often posing next to it as photographs are taken.

The shadows of evening were slowly but surely drawing in, a clear indication that night was fast approaching. We quickly realised that it was time to say goodbye to the faithful people of Holy Trinity. We walked on the path along the canal leading to Lancaster – a distance of 4.2 miles.

By this time, we were ready for something to eat after a long day of walking, praying and sharing our experience with God's people in fine churches and with people along the way. We then decided to have our evening tea at a restaurant in Lancaster town centre, which took about an hour and a half, and then we made our way up Castle Hill to Lancaster Priory for the closing service of our day, which was due to start at 7.30 pm. Arriving there at about 7.00 pm, it was a welcome break to sit down and stretch our tired legs while reflecting candidly on the day. Sam was suffering from blisters he'd incurred during the nineteen-mile walk. The Archdeacon of Blackburn, the Venerable John Hawley, offered sympathetically to go and buy some special plasters from the chemist to soothe the pain. It was an offer that Sam had no hesitation in accepting!

The service, which started promptly, was structured to conclude the events of the day. It was an inspiring service with all the neces-sary spiritual ingredients that brought a flood of blessing to me. I was highly touched and felt humbled when the archdeacon compared Geoff, Sam and myself to Shadrach, Meshach and Abednego – a moving biblical story which dominates Daniel chapter 3. The Re-vised Standard Version calls the three faithful and prayerful men 'God's heroes'. After the service ended, a vote of thanks was uttered to those concerned and we finally made our way home, arriving at 9.00 pm.

On my way home I couldn't help but observe the sheer beauty of Lancaster. A comparatively small city, it has an exceptionally vibrant culture. Both Lancaster and Cumbria universities, which stand on a ridge just outside the town centre, have given great impetus to its value. Lancaster possesses some of the finest buildings in the north-west. Among them is the castle, with part of it used as a pris-on, and the famous Ashton Memorial which has become a familiar sight for travellers on the M6 motorway. It was originally built for Lord Ashton, who made a fortune from linoleum and oilcloth in the late nineteenth century. This unique building is the centrepiece of Williamson Park, where it stands on top of a steep hill and is usu-ally seen as a viewpoint towards the Lakeland fells, as well as other places like Blackpool, Fleetwood, Morecambe and Heysham. The park's other attractions include a tropical butterfly house and, in the summer time, a promenade theatre production, which draws people from a large area.

The origin of Lancaster itself goes right back to the Neolithic period and, following the Roman occupation, it has been highly developed and prosperous. In fact, for a few glorious years in the mid eighteenth century, it became Britain's second port. Of course, Lancaster has the great advantage of sitting comfortably between the coast and the hills, and is surrounded by lovely countryside and the famous River Lune which flows into the sea.

Chapter 6

DAY TWO
MONDAY 25 MAY

Garstang
Broughton
Goosnargh
Longridge

Forth in Thy Name, O Lord I go. My daily labour to pursue. Thee, only thee resolved to know, in all I think or speak or do. Give me to bear thy easy yoke and every moment watch and pray; and still to things eternal look, and hasten to Thy glorious day.
(Charles Wesley, 1707–78)

After a good night's rest in the comfort of our homes, Sam kept his promise and picked me up in the minibus at 8.00 am and, without wasting any time, we quickly made our way once again to pick Geoff up from Shireshead Vicarage at Forton. The traffic between the two homes was not too busy, which allowed us to arrive at 8.15 am. Within minutes, Geoff, who was expecting us around that time, casually strolled along the road to the bus, wearing his shorts, as he had done the day before, being encouraged by the nice weather.

We left almost immediately to travel to Garstang, where prior arrangements had been made to meet at St Thomas' Church for prayer at 9.00 am. The incumbent, Reverend Michael Gisbourne, who was clearly pleased by our arrival, welcomed us and introduced us to a group of people who came to join us in prayer. It was quite obvious that he had been waiting in anticipation of intercession for an important building project that was in the pipeline, as well as other church matters, for which we were happy to participate in the prayer session.

Afterwards, I was given a one-page information sheet explaining how the present church was originally built in 1769 as a chapel attached to St Helen's Church, and has since developed considerably to become St Thomas' Parish Church in its own right, in 1878, with its own mission statement as follows:

> We seek to proclaim the Kingdom of God and to make the good news of Christ more fully known through worship, service and witness. Growing strong in faith and love, we work together to serve and care for all.

I was very impressed with St Thomas' Church, which is placed as a light in the centre of the market town of Garstang. It is said that presently the church is a thriving community, welcoming people of all ages to worship. There are many flourishing groups, including the Sunday school, new youth group, Mothers' Union, ladies' group, men's fellowship and the Supper Club. All of these provide ideal opportunities for people to get involved and to get to know each other in a relaxed and social atmosphere.

The church is proud to demonstrate that the highlight of their week is worship, with a group of people who take the Christian faith seriously and enjoy worshipping Jesus, believing that Christianity is about a personal relationship with God and with others.

Subsequently, we set off on our walk to Broughton with six people accompanying us. Being Bank Holiday Monday, the road in part was rather busy so we decided to walk alongside the canal bank; a distance of 7.1 miles. Like the canal between Kendal and Morecambe, this canal has a long history for recreational purposes, such as canoeing, swimming, fishing and so on.

The task of praying whilst walking along this beautiful stretch of canal on a nice sunny day was by no means easy, as we were repeatedly distracted by people taking their dogs for walks, as well as the occasional ducks with their young ones swimming on the still water. Some members of the team inevitably drew my attention to the smooth, stylish way the swans swim. To the naked eye it seems almost motionless, yet in reality they get from point A to point B very quickly. We virtually stopped to admire the mysterious movement of the swans and their cygnets (see photograph). At times like this I am reminded of the hymn 'All Things Bright and Beautiful'. Taking into consideration our observation of the creatures, the glorious scenery along the canal bank with the pretty wild flowers, and the green grassy tracks, it is worth recalling this appropriate hymn:

> All things bright and beautiful
> All creatures great and small
> All things wise and wonderful
> The Lord God made them all.
>
> Each little flower that opens
> Each little bird that sings
> He made their glowing colours
> He made their tiny wings.
>
> The purple-headed mountain
> the river running by
> The sunset and the morning
> that brightens up the sky.
>
> The cold wind in the winter
> The pleasant summer sun
> the ripe fruits in the garden
> He made them every one.
>
> The tall trees in the green wood
> The meadows for our play
> The rushes by the water
> To gather every day.
>
> He gave us eyes to see them
> And lips that we might tell
> How great is God Almighty
> Who has made all things well.
> (Mrs C.F. Alexander, 1818–95)

This inspiring hymn is supported by scriptural verses. For example, Genesis 1:24: 'And God said, "Let the earth bring forth living creatures according to their kinds ... " And it was so' (RSV). Also Psalm 1:1–3 seals it magnificently in the words: 'Blessed is the man who walks not in the counsel of the wicked ... but his delight is in the law of the LORD, and on his law he meditates day and night. He is like a tree planted by streams of water, that yields its fruit in its season, and its leaf does not wither. In all that he does, he prospers' (RSV).

By then we had been walking for about three long hours when we suddenly discovered that it was fast approaching our lunch time. In the process we made a brief stop at Barton Grange Garden Centre to eat our sandwiches. The large garden centre was recently built with a huge café, store and several attractions – among them, surprisingly, is the men's toilet which has specially designed floral urinals, a must-see for many visitors! The management consider them so special that they even display the pictures of the designed units at the entrance. As a result, both men and women do go in to have a look. Even the bishop couldn't resist the temptation to go and pay a visit!

The people at St John's Church in Broughton were expecting us to arrive on their premises at 12.00 noon, but the stop we made at the garden centre delayed our journey, which caused us to arrive at the church at 12.45 pm. As we were approaching the church with less than a mile to go, we met with some of the church people on a rescue mission. They were so concerned after the arrival time had expired that they were coming to see what had happened, so we happily spent the last few hundred yards walking alongside them, at the same time giving an explanation of what had happened, and sharing our experience of the walk with them.

Arriving under the roof of St John's was a welcome break, with some refreshments prepared for us which we thoroughly enjoyed.

Afterwards we participated in a short service which was organised by the incumbent, Reverend Sidney Fox. Ten cheerful members of the congregation joined us in this formal service. Amongst the matters for prayer was a major renovation project launched in 2006 as part of the Diocesan Mission Plan. The project identified five phases of work, from the tower roof repairs to interior redecoration, and the total estimated cost amounted to £231,000.

The church square tower was established in 1533 during the reign of King Henry Vlll and it is one of the oldest buildings in the Preston area still in daily use. The building is located approximately 180 metres east of the A6 north of Preston on the northerly bank of Blundel Brook. I was amazed to hear that they had a contingent of sixty-five to seventy members in the choir.

A stretch of three miles separates Broughton from Goosnargh, where we headed next accompanied by three members of the church, with one of the members, Sheila, insisting in taking her dog, Philie. Due to the fast-moving motorway between Broughton and Goosnargh we were advised to travel there via a field. Fortunately, two of the local men who accompanied us were part of a local club who walk periodically in the area, so they knew of a short cut in the field, but the passage was rather muddy and rough. We took the risk to trail along the short cut knowing what to expect. What we were not told before was the challenge of climbing over a number of fences, with some of them rather awkward to get over. However, we were amused for a brief moment when the dog, Philie, spotted a rabbit and, without prior warning, decided to chase after it. When we came to the next open field the dog met his match with a group of cows which didn't like dogs. They chased after Philie, who was clearly motivated by fear – and ran for security near the owner's feet. This in turn made the cows head towards us, which caused me to be worried until we safely arrived near the next fence and quickly jumped over.

After walking for 3.9 miles we came to the picturesque village of Goosnargh which lies between Broughton and Longridge. Standing in the centre of Goosnargh is the church of St Mary, where we met with the incumbent, Reverend Jeff Finch, who greeted us with a smile. Some of the members were busy preparing refreshments for us at the back of the church.

After our adventure across the muddy field it was good to be walking on the solid road surface once again. However, I do not wish to dismiss the enticing views of the wild flowers, plants and trembling trees we saw along the way. In fact, it was part of the challenge cheerfully accomplished for the day.

The ministry of the church in the Fellside area parishes is undertaken by a ministry team which is composed of both ordained clergy and lay workers. The bishop licensed workers to particular ministries to communicate the gospel message in both words and deeds.

We enjoyed sharing with the group present about our journey so far and we couldn't resist telling them about our unusual experience across the fields, which prompted some amusement. We then prayed with the group inside the church, followed by refreshments, and afterwards departed from there to our next destination.

Our final stop was at St Paul's with St Lawrence's Church in Longridge, where a main meal was prepared for us before the closing service of the day, organised by the vicar, Reverend David Anderson. We had an enjoyable meal cooked by David's wife, Claire. After eating I felt like going to bed for a good sleep, but before contemplating that we had to attend the formal evening service, and each of us shared our experience of the walk and the aims and objectives of walking the long distance.

One of the chosen hymns that touched me deeply in the church and was reproduced in their church magazine was the inspiring hymn 'Servant Song' based on Mark 9:35 (lyrics and tune written by Richard Gillard in New Zealand in 1976–77), with the beautiful yet relevant words:

Brother, let me be your servant
Let me be as Christ to you.
Pray that I may have the grace
To let you be my servant, too.

We are pilgrims on a journey
We are brothers on the road.
We are here to help each other
Walk the mile and bear the load.

I will hold the Christlight for you
In the night-time of your fear.
I will hold my hand out to you
Speak the peace you long to hear.

I will weep when you are weeping
When you laugh, I will laugh with you.
I will share your joy and sorrow
Till we have seen this journey through.

When we sing to God in heaven
We shall find such harmony.
Born of all we have known together
Of Christ's love and agony.

The story of St Lawrence goes right back to 1450 where it started
with the dedication of a chapel. Reference is made to the Chapel
of St Lawrence in 1546. (It is interesting to note that in between
this crucial period, King Henry Vlll became the figurehead of the
Church of England, in 1529.) Having survived this period of reformation in England, it was rebuilt in 1784 and a school erected in
1731. In 1668 the church was officially established as the ecclesiastical parish of Longridge.

The church's mission is to share the good news of God's love
through worship, friendship and prayer. It is engaged in an ecumenical set-up in Longridge with the Roman Catholic, Methodist
and the United Reformed Church. The group is known as Churches
Together in Longridge and have been working together now for
many years, sharing in various ways. This unity among the churches
has had a tremendous impact on the local community. It is said that
there is a more positive feeling within the community and a greater
understanding of the different traditions as a whole.

We felt the community spirit both outside and inside the church.
Perhaps this explains why there were so many at the closing service
of the day. The service, which was well structured, finished between
8.00 and 9.00 pm. A banquet was prepared for us in a hall adjacent
to the church, with lots of food – specially made cakes and drink.
We ate as much as we could, with plenty left over. This reminds me
very much of the feeding of the 5,000, illustrated in John 6, with
particular emphasis on verses 11 to 13: 'Jesus then took the loaves,
gave thanks, and distributed to those who were seated as much as
they wanted. He did the same with the fish. When they had all had
enough to eat, he said to his disciples, "Gather the pieces that are
left over. Let nothing be wasted." So they gathered them and filled
twelve baskets with the pieces of the five barley loaves left over by
those who had eaten' (NIV).

Incidentally, we had a miniature carbon copy of this incident (not
the miracle!). After everybody had eaten enough there was plenty of
food left over, so a couple of the ladies who were feeling generous

wrapped a fair amount for me to put in my bag to take with me for our next journey.

Mrs Jean Pearson, the bishop's wife, came to pick us up to take us home at the end of a glorious day. We left Longridge between 9.00 and 10.00 pm and made our way back to Lancaster to prepare for the next day.

Chapter 7

DAY THREE
TUESDAY 26 MAY

Clitheroe
Whalley
Fence
Nelson
Colne

*Night and day we pray most earnestly that we may see you again and supply
what is lacking in your faith.*
(1 Thessalonians 3:10, NIV)

The fourteen-mile walk the previous day seemed to have geared
our bodies for a good night's sleep at home. As expected, the
night went by very quickly, but the few hours spent at home were
quality time before Sam picked me up at 7.30 am, allowing ten minutes to pick up Geoff at 8.00 am.

We then travelled to Clitheroe, a journey of 4.1 miles, which
took about one hour, arriving at St James' Church at 9.00 am, to
be greeted by the rector, Reverend Mark Pickett, together with a
group of church members, who came to support us and to share in
the morning service organised by the incumbent, with a focus on
our walk.

St James' Church has a lively fellowship with a style of worship that is very informal and contemporary. Emphasis is placed on solid Bible-based teaching, which is applied both in Sunday services as well as in midweek study groups. The church aims to serve the community at large through a range of activities for all ages. It also works and shares in collaboration with other Christian agencies at home and abroad, through financial support and personal involvement.

Our task having been completed in Clitheroe, we made our way to Whalley, accompanied by two walkers from the church, Jasper and Gill. Meanwhile, Sam drove the bus to the abbey and came back to meet us on his bicycle.

The journey between Clitheroe and Whalley on foot was not easy, due to the narrow side path along the main road. There were times when we had to be ever so careful, with oncoming vehicles pounding the road at high speed and causing waves of dust from the dry road to rise up in the air, inevitably invading us.

It was a big blessing to have had Jasper – whom I personally knew during my time in Clitheroe as an actor in the town's famous Mystery Play – and Gill walking with us to the abbey, educating us with the local history as well as sharing their own Christian faith with us.

Midway between Clitheroe and Whalley we encountered a frightening episode which was highly alarming. While we were praying and marching down the road with our minds focused on our plans, suddenly a car pulled up and stopped very near to us, and the driver asked, in a commanding voice: 'What is your occupation?' We all rather jumped for a moment. In answer to this direct question, issued in such an abrupt manner, Bishop Geoff quickly stepped forward to about a foot from the driver, and replied with an authoritative voice, 'I am the bishop, and we are praying on the way.' I then drew near to the men sitting in the back of the car, which had the window wound down, and asked, 'Is there anything we can pray for you or your family?' One of them replied, 'Pray that the pubs open earlier' and they drove off at high speed.

After the brief encounter with the four men, we quickly discovered what had actually happened. They were all workmen wearing yellow jackets, and we were wearing yellow jackets as well. We understood that they had lost some of their work colleagues and were desperately looking for them, so immediately, when they saw the yellow jackets, they automatically assumed that the missing pieces in their jigsaw had been found. But they were wrong. What they couldn't see was the writing on the back of our yellow jackets which said 'Praying Around', with the illustration of a map, so their puzzle remained unsolved, while we continued on our journey to St Mary's and All Saints Church in Whalley.

At St Mary's Church we received a warm welcome by the warden, who gave us a brief explanation of the parish situation and some matters for prayer. I was rather impressed with a special support service they were preparing for, 'Back to Church Sunday', 27 September 2009. They had some very creative ideas for people to wear jeans for the service to make it relevant for the occasion, believing that doing something different would attract more people to the church.

They were also busy preparing programmes aimed at parents in the day school of 300 children. From my own experience of day school linked with the church, it has never been easy to reach and attract children and their parents to Christ. Nevertheless, endless efforts still have to be made to carry out the mission of God and the church of Christ into the day school.

St Mary's Church is literally a few hundred yards from Whalley Abbey, so we headed towards the abbey after we had prayed in the church.

Whalley Abbey

On arrival at Whalley Abbey, we were joyfully greeted by the warden who was pleased to see us. Of course, I am no stranger to Whalley Abbey, as I performed in the Mystery Play, directed by Mrs Margaret Smith, on more than one occasion.

Whalley Abbey has a long history which is quite interesting. It was founded in the year 1296 by a group of Cistercian monks from the county of Cheshire. (Incidentally, I was one of the actors who played the part of a Cistercian monk in 2000. Reflecting on the Cistercian monk's habit I wore on the day brought back happy memories as I walked through the abbey gate.)

The order itself was founded by St Robert of Molesme (1027–1111) as an offshoot of the Benedictine Order which was already in existence. History records that the Mother House was at Cleaux in

France, where the Order inherited its name. The abbey is noted for its remains, which includes part of the Chapter House and a fourteenth-century gateway. It must have been a painful experience to watch as such a beautiful abbey was destroyed mercilessly during the Reformation in England. However, many of the stones were used in local churches, farms and houses.

From Whalley Abbey we travelled to St Anne's Church in Fence, where Reverend Richard Adams serves as incumbent. After experiencing some difficulties in finding the church building, we eventually discovered it with a little help from at least a couple of people who we stopped on the road to ask for directions.

St Anne's Church is one of three Christian churches situated in this fine village of Fence, to serve the local community in an ecumenical set-up – what they described as a 'demonstration of the reality of God in our life'.

The Church of St Anne has struggled to grow, but the church leadership has been greatly encouraged by the increasing numbers of families attending the monthly family service. Encouraged by this sign of growth, improved facilities had to be created to accommodate people more comfortably.

After visiting the church and talking to people individually, it was clear that there is a real focus on community involvement. From what I understood, the church serves the local community through the combination of the skills and enthusiastic interest of the church members.

Having shared and prayed with them, we departed for St Paul, Little Marsden in Nelson, a distance of 5.7 miles. Thankfully, one of the church members who had a comprehensive knowledge of the area and of the location of churches there came along with us to the next church to be visited. This proved to be indispensable.

By now we had already covered about fifty miles on the long journey and we were just about to face one of the biggest challenges on the way; a long hill that seemed to have no end to it. I had been warned before that the Burnley area was rather hilly, but I never realised that it included Nelson, Colne and Briercliffe to that extent. After leaving Fence, we casually strolled down the road leading to Nelson until we came across a little hill which we happily climbed to the peak, not realising that this was a taster with the main course to come. From the top of this little hill we took a long look at the other side. We could see with the naked eye the stark beauty of the place. In the midst of this majestic view, I managed to spot the spire of a peaceful church standing on top of this gigantic hill. For a brief moment I thought, in my enquiring mind, could it possibly be the church that we are going to visit? My fears were soon to be realised when our companion pointed with his finger to a church near to the one I had noticed. He suggested to us for very good reasons that it would be better going through the field to avoid the winding road, which was rather dangerous with numerous vehicles speeding along.

After pausing for a moment to consider his suggestion, we accepted it without contention and hurriedly made our way across the waiting field. Passing through a small gate we arrived at the bottom of the hill where the town centre is situated, ready for the ascent of another lengthy hill.

We started the climb boldly and with full confidence to get to the top, which we thankfully did, with a running sweat.

When we got there, I could see a breathtaking view right across the other side of the town centre, which I could only summarise in one word – 'spectacular'.

In some ways this long and steep hill, as glorious as the scenery might have been, was symbolic of our epic journey around the diocese. Up until now we had been walking for three long days with another five to go. I reflected on the place where we started at Silverdale and thought that the progress made had been very impressive, so I must press on with my mind fixed on the Lord, while the prayer and fellowship kept me occupied in looking upward and forward rather than backward and downward.

Recalling the words of the apostle Paul in Philippians 3:13,14 he asserts: ' ... forgetting what lies behind and straining forward to what lies ahead, I press on towards the goal for the prize of the heavenly call of God in Christ Jesus' (NRSV).

When Paul wrote these inspiring words, he had an amazing record of past achievements in many of the towns and cities he had already visited in the Roman Empire, yet he was able to say with confidence that he was leaving his past achievements behind and pushing forward with present determination.

Similarly, I refused to allow the past experience of the lengthy hill to torture my mind, but we pressed on to Colne, arriving at St Batholomew's Church at 6.00 pm. This time we were fortunate enough to be accompanied by two clergymen, Reverend Tony Rindl and Reverend Alan Jones and other members of the church, plus a dog called Sky, belonging to one of our companions – a very friendly dog which appeared to have been well trained to adapt easily to strangers.

As we walked along, we prayed outside other churches and institutions, for example, St John's and St Philip's. Some of the churches we saw along the way had sadly been closed down for worship but were being used for other activities. Arriving in Colne was quite an amazing experience, as we witnessed an elaborate celebration by nearly the whole of the town, which was acknowledging Burnley Football Club's promotion from the Championship Division. There were flags hanging on a number of buildings, including pubs and clubs. Vehicles were blowing their horns and nearly everyone in the area was talking about the club's promotion.

Colne town stands on the River Henburn near the Leeds and Liverpool canal, about five and a half miles north-east of Burnley. St Bartholomew's Church, Colne sits at the summit of the hill on which the town is built, at a height of 623 feet above sea level. Records show that the church existed in 1122 and during the reign of Henry I, when Hugh de Ca Val granted it to the Priory of Pontefract. It was restored and enlarged in 1857.

Presently it is involved in a Team Ministry and has a vibrant ministry under the leadership of the rector, Reverend Tony Rindl. The church has been modernised to create a coffee bar at the back by removing some of the pews to allow room for socialisation and refreshments.

After a delicious meal served to us in the coffee bar area, we moved literally a few feet away to the main church for the 7.30 pm service, specially arranged to highlight the end of our walk for the day. It was a lively time of worship led by a modern worship group with a reasonable number of the congregation present. As usual, Geoff, Sam and I shared and prayed with the congregation. Then we retired to the Reverend Tony Rindl's vicarage at Skipton Road, Foulridge, where we slept for the night in preparation for the next day.

Chapter 8

DAY FOUR
WEDNESDAY 27 MAY

Briercliffe

Burnley

Accrington

Baxenden

Evening and morning and at noon I will pray, and cry aloud, And He shall hear my voice.
(Psalm 55:17, NKJV)

It has been rightly said in the past over and over again that the English weather is unpredictable and this saying proved to be right on Wednesday! After three days of glorious weather, with the hot sun blazing on us to the extent that Bishop Geoff had no problem wearing his shorts, suddenly the weather, which seemed to be saying to us 'You have all had enough of this!', changed considerably.

Following our breakfast at Foulridge Vicarage, when we were making preparation to leave for Briercliffe, suddenly we heard this continuous sound. I had my suspicions that it could be rain, but I had to look outside to confirm my fear. This was the point when options had to be weighed carefully. Two choices were open to us; one was to go, or we could wait for the rain to be over and then set off. After a careful inspection of the weather conditions, there appeared no obvious signs that it would stop shortly, judging by the colour of the clouds, and the general atmosphere. With this pressing on our minds, we decided to proceed in the rain, as we were expected to arrive at St James' Church in Briercliffe at 9.00 am.

The apostle Paul may have had extensive knowledge and experience of these sort of weather conditions when he said to young Timothy in his second letter to him: "In the presence of God and of Christ Jesus, who will judge the living and the dead, and in view of his appearing and his kingdom, I give you this charge: Preach the Word; be prepared in season and out of season; correct, rebuke and encourage – with great patience and careful instruction' (2 Timothy 4:1,2, NIV).

Thankfully we arrived at Briercliffe as planned and were cheerfully greeted by the incumbent, Reverend Rachel Watts. Despite the rain and endless hills, we kept to our time schedule.

Briercliffe is three miles north-east of Burnley and has an interesting history. Until very recently, Briercliffe's main claim to historic fame has been the concentration of prehistoric remains which were reported to be found on the higher land in the east side of the parish. Evidence shows that the excavation took place in the nineteenth century, and some of the objects can be viewed at Towneley Hall in Burnley.

The area is popular for walking because of the Pennine Way. In fact, the combination of the moorland countryside, the prehistoric remains, its museum, interesting walking facilities and its industrial archaeological wealth has made Briercliffe quite an attractive place to visit.

The church itself is dedicated to St James the Great and dates back to 1841. The church receives excellent support from the local community. I counted sixty-six adverts from local agencies in the parish magazine, occupying forty-one pages. I was pleased to see St James Lanehead School motto read: 'At our school we aim to provide a caring Christian learning environment which values children as individuals and encourages them to fulfil their potential and become responsible and active members of God's world.'

Despite the weather conditions, it was time to move on to our next station at St Andrew's, Burnley, where we were due to arrive at 10.30 am, which we managed comfortably. Arriving in Burnley at a time when the feeling of excitement was still very high, with the results of Burnley Football Club's successful promotion, made me wonder what kind of reception we would get. The reception, as one would have guessed, was revolving around the club's achievements and what it meant for their future. Everywhere we turned people were engaged in conversation about football. We were told that on the Monday evening when they played that crucial game at Wembley Stadium, nearly all the people who were able went from Burnley – so much so that they ran out of buses and coaches in Burnley, and had to go elsewhere in Lancashire to hire lots of coaches to make up the numbers.

We were highly honoured to have the Bishop of Burnley, the Rt Reverend John Goddard, Canon Tom Bill, Canon Peter Hapgood-Strickland and a few other members walking with us for a reasonable distance in the Burnley area. We had a pleasant walk along the parish of St Andrew's and St Peter's. The area has been described as UPA. The term 'UPA' by definition means Urban Priority Area, as differentiated from suburban. In defining the term 'UPA', it is recognised from the 1981 census that the Department of Environment stipulates that an area with all or most of the following characteristics would be officially classified as an Urban Priority Area:

• An area with a high level of unemployment;
• There are a large number of old people living alone;
• Where there are a mixture of people from several ethnic backgrounds;
• If there are over-crowded homes;
• Where there are homes lacking basic amenities;
• Where there are large numbers of single-parent families.

As for St Peter's Church where we visited, it was first mentioned in a Charter of 1122 and rebuilt in 1533, and over the years several additions and renovation work has been carried out there.

We were blessed with the presence of some members of the congregation of St Peter's Church joining us and, like the church members of St Andrew's which we had visited an hour earlier, they shared with us and passed on some useful information for prayer, which we treated as confidential.

After prayer and refreshments, we made our way to Accrington. With the rain having abated by now we managed to arrive at St Augustine with St John's Church in Accrington at 2.30 pm, which had no incumbent at the time of our visit. Nevertheless, we were warmly welcomed by members of the congregation who looked after us very well and passed on necessary information for prayer.

Both parishes in Accrington are situated primarily in Urban Priority Areas, where they are affected by deprivation. Judging by what I saw in the Accrington areas, it is obvious that they have been hit by the recession, which of course is a national problem with the present economic climate.

An hour later, we went across to St James' in Cannon Street, Accrington where Reverend David Lyon is the Team Rector. St James' is a Grade II listed building and has been described as an 'historic Accrington icon'. A church has existed on the site since 1544, but the present church was rebuilt in the 1800s. The small but faithful congregation is developing its ministry to the town centre community, and realises that the church should be open on weekdays when the area is alive with people. To this end they are going to employ a development worker who will help the congregation to reorder the church so that it may be used as a centre for celebrating music in all its forms.

The town of Accrington itself lies at the foot of Hameldon Hill to the east and south of Haslingden Hills. A century ago it was a small, insignificant village which the historians described as a 'considerable village', but over the years it has seen many changes.

In order to keep to our time schedule for 6.00 pm at St John's Church, we moved on to Baxenden which we made with about ten minutes to spare. The incumbent, Reverend Joe Fielder, came to meet us at the church, accompanied by a young couple and a dog called Gordon, with instructions about the evening service and accommodation for the night. It was the last stop of the day, after approximately eighteen miles of walking.

Each one of us was allocated to a home in the parish. I was pleasantly surprised to find that my host was a former member of St Andrew's Church in Livesey, Blackburn where I had served as curate. I had not seen her for about thirty years, but before catching up with our news we were summoned to the church building for an elaborate meal prepared by some members of the congregation, with a large number joining us. Amongst them was a young couple, husband and wife, who came to the feast as a result of hearing the news on the radio. I was sitting at the same table as this couple, which gave me an ideal opportunity to tell them about the Christian faith, and to encourage them to go to church, which would make a difference to their lives.

After a delicious meal we had our usual closing church service for the day, led by a lively worship group, with the vicar officiating at the main service itself. Again, as the three of us had done so many times before, we shared our experience of the journey with them, which was highly appreciated. Following an extemporary time of prayer with the congregation, we retired gracefully to various homes.

Ann and her husband, Jack Brown, were delighted to have me for the evening with them. They looked after me very well, and we were able to catch up with as much news as possible. Ann's dad and mum, Mr and Mrs Fox, whom I knew very well when I served in the parish they attended, had passed away. Ann concluded by saying that her mother and father would have been very pleased to know that they provided me with lodging for the night!

St John's foundation was laid and consecrated in 1818. The site was a market garden which was purchased from the Town Council to build the church. It was designed by William Buran, a famous architect at the time. St John's (where, incidentally, I preached over a decade ago) is a church with vision. It has various projects under active consideration which aim to equip and help the congregation to fulfil St John's Church mission in the twenty-first century.

Chapter 9

DAY FIVE
THURSDAY 28 MAY

Blackburn
Darwen
Standish
Chorley
Whittle-le-Woods

Great is the LORD, and greatly to be praised
In the city of our God,
In His holy mountain.
Beautiful in elevation,
The joy of all the earth,
Is Mount Zion on the sides of the north,
The city of the great King.
(Psalm 48:1,2, NKJV)

The apostle Paul found that it was extremely hard to say farewell to the people whom he visited in Ephesus, often spending some Christian quality time with them. In fact, his deep inner feeling is expressed as we read: 'After this Paul stayed many days longer, and then took leave of the brethren and sailed for Syria, and with him Priscilla and Aquila. ... And they came to Ephesus and he left them there; but he himself went into the synagogue and argued with the Jews. When they asked him to stay for a longer period, he declined; but on taking leave of them he said, "I will return to you if God wills," and he set sail from Ephesus' (Acts 18:18–21, RSV).

I was reminded in some ways of Paul's leaving Ephesus. After a restful night sleeping in a comfortable bed, it was time to say goodbye to my former parishioners. I wanted to stay longer but, like Paul, who had many places to visit and had to go, we still had twenty-two more churches in nineteen cities, towns and villages. So I gathered my things, packed my suitcase and prayed for the family. Within minutes, Sam arrived in the bus to pick me up. At that point I had a quick glance at my watch: 8.00 am.

As I answered the front door to Sam, I saw outside was already saturated, soon to be followed by another heavy shower. My host, who was obviously feeling sorry for me, offered me a pair of plastic waterproof trousers – an offer that I could not resist, to save me getting wet. She explained that they were relatively new, which caused me to feel a little bit reluctant, leaving with her precious property; so much so that I offered to return them to her at my earliest convenience, but she insisted that it didn't matter and I shouldn't worry about it as she would rather see me go with them rather than get wet in the heavy rain. For this and for her generosity in the way she fed and looked after me, I thanked her most sincerely. Then I left with Sam to go to pick up Geoff at St John's vicarage, which is located on a little hill about half a mile away from where we set off. Our next visit was to St Luke's with St Philip's Church at Bank Top in Blackburn.

I have some happy memories of Blackburn, where I lived for thirty years, and in particular, served as priest in charge and vicar of St Barnabas Church for twenty-seven years, so we had no problem finding our destination. Blackburn has a fascinating history as a local market and fervent religious centre which dates back to Norman times. It is noted for its early growth of textile industry production in the seventeenth century, and rapid industrial development in the eighteenth century that transformed it into a leading industrial town in Lancashire. It is well known that the Blackburn town became one of the world's leading centres for cotton production.

However, as the cotton industry diminished, the cotton mills were demolished and this inevitably brought a striking alteration to Blackburn as a whole. The impact has made a dramatic difference, with a comprehensive development of a modern town centre as well as the implementation of a massive housing programme, which is designed to demolish unfit houses and replace them with modern new ones. In recent years, Blackburn has been seeing these changes that are fundamental to the town's appearance. I left there only about eight months ago and when I passed through Blackburn on the walk, I was pleasantly surprised to see recent changes that have taken place.

Walking through what was once the ancient market town of Blackburn, with the thought of visiting several churches marked on our waiting list in the vicinity, reminds me very much of the apostle Paul in Acts 18:23: 'After spending some time there he departed and went from place to place through the region of Galatia and Phrygia, strengthening all the disciples' (NRSV).

Arriving promptly at 9.00 am at St Luke's Church, it was pleasing to find that the incumbent, Reverend Fleur Green, together with some of the church officials, were already standing in a straight line like well-trained soldiers, ready to greet us. After a friendly Christian greeting, we got down to the serious business of united prayer, which went very well.

St Luke's Church is literally a few yards away from St Wilfrid's Church of England Secondary School and College of Technology in Duckworth Street. In the past, the incumbent of the church has served as chaplain to the school. Above all, the church as a whole has a responsibility to carry out the mission of our Lord into the school; even more so because the school has a very good reputation which, as a result, makes it extremely popular. Children come from a large area in Lancashire to attend it.

St Wilfrid's School was founded on a strong Christian ethos and maintains a high Christian, moral and educational standard. In fact, Ofsted concluded in their assessment that 'This is a good school with outstanding features'. The school administration advocates that they are committed to safeguarding and promoting the welfare of children and young people, and expects all the members of their staff and volunteers to share this commitment. It is therefore important for St Luke's Church to continue its involvement in this successful and highly regarded school.

After our experience in climbing endless hills in Briercliffe, Colne and Burnley, one would have thought that there surely couldn't be any more steep hills in the diocese. Such thoughts might have been greeted with the word 'wrong', as we were just about to face another challenge of a long hill known as Jack Walker Way, after departing from St Luke's Church to visit St Bartholomew's Church; a distance of approximately three miles.

St Bartholomew's happens to be sitting right on the top of the hill. Symbolically speaking one could say that because of the position where it is placed, it represents a spiritual light shining on top of the hill overlooking the valley. With its high summit, it offers panoramic views classified as areas of outstanding natural beauty. I could imagine that when people go up to the church to worship and look around this inspirational view, they must think of the God of creation who, by His power, brought all these beautiful things into existence. This is captured magnificently in the words of the psalm: 'Let the mountains bear prosperity for the people, and the hills, in righteousness ... Blessed be the LORD, the God of Israel, who alone does wondrous things. Blessed be his glorious name for ever; may his glory fill the whole earth! Amen and Amen' (Psalm 72:3,18,19, RSV).

Having conquered the hill successfully, we were joyfully greeted by one lonely lady who had been patiently waiting for us to arrive. Up to this point, we had already visited twenty-two churches, and it was the first time that we had witnessed the presence of only one person to meet and share with us. Amazingly, in all the places we'd visited, there were people who knew me and, for the first time, after four and a half days of walking, this lady – in response to a question put to her by one of my two colleagues – said that she didn't know me. By now it had become a topic for discussion that everywhere we went, people knew Herrick! However, this official was kind enough to show us around the new worship area. Walking in through the swinging doors, my heart was captivated by the architectural beauty of this modern church. The inside is built in an unusual style; it was probably built this way deliberately to be different from the traditional-looking church, and partly because of the school involvement as well. One can only assume that the designer of the church would have thought very deeply in planning it in this fashion, to stimulate its members for modern worship.

St Bartholomew's used to be on Bolton Road next to Blackburn Rovers football ground, but the congregation moved to modern new premises after the closure of the former building. St Bartholomew's has joined with the Church of the Saviour to form the 'Benefice of the Redeemer', and they share the same mission statement: 'Seeking to know Christ and to make Christ better known'. They do share in other ways, and it is said that St Bartholomew's people are encouraged to use their skills or gifts for the service of God in the world.

It was time to reluctantly turn our backs on my beloved Blackburn (I met my wife and got married there, and three of my children were born and grew up in Blackburn. I also made many friends during my thirty years' ministry in two churches.) We wondered whether we should proceed to the north to visit St James' Church, standing on top of a huge hill, or follow the road on the east leading to Darwen.

Like every good and loyal clergy member of the Church of England, we inevitably decided to have a meeting about it. (Clergymen are used to having regular meetings in the Church of England, so much so that it has been said repeatedly that some of them suffer with a disease called 'meetingitis'; no one suffers the consequences more than their wives, many of whom have complained bitterly about this malady.)

After a short deliberation meeting, without any minutes being taken, we unanimously agreed to travel towards the east to St Cuthbert's in Darwen. The event that follows convinced me beyond a shadow of a doubt that the Lord was leading us in this direction. On the way, we felt the need to stop and pray outside Darwen Vale Secondary School. By now we were already in the habit of praying outside institutions and buildings which we considered of any marked significance, so Darwen Vale School was no exception. The difference was that I knew from inside knowledge that Darwen Vale was experiencing many problems in the school sector, so there were plenty of reasons for a good session of prayer.

Our decision to change course seemed to mirror Paul's decision to change course on his second missionary journey, when the Holy Spirit spoke to him and led him to his next post:

'And when they had come opposite Mysia, they attempted to go into Bithynia, but the Spirit of Jesus did not allow them; so, passing by Mysia, they went down to Troas. And a vision appeared to Paul in the night: a man of Macedonia was standing beseeching him and saying, "Come over to Macedonia and help us." And when he had seen the vision, immediately we sought to go on into Macedonia, concluding that God had called us to preach the gospel to them' (Acts 16:7–10, RSV).

A few days later, I received a message from a member of the staff at Darwen Vale School who excitedly said to me that the situation in school had suddenly got better, and related several areas of improvement which had encouraged her, but she didn't know why this sudden change in circumstances had taken place. This gave me a golden opportunity to break the news that three clergymen had prayed outside the school during their walk to Darwen town. She was very pleased and thanked me. I in turn passed on the good news of answered prayer to my two colleagues.

St Cuthbert's Church in Darwen, where we were due next, is about two miles from Darwen Vale School. As we approached the traditional ancient-looking church, we spotted the figure of a well-built, sturdy-looking man with some photographic equipment standing outside the church. Judging by his movements, the equipment and the busy way he was fussing about, we had no problem in identifying him as a reporter from the *Lancashire Evening Telegraph*, who looked like a hunting member of the paparazzi, seeking his prey. He in turn had no difficulty in recognising us to be the three walkers whom he had been patiently waiting for. Without wasting any time, he started giving us instructions in preparation to take appropriate photographs.

'I want you to walk along the roadside on the right facing me,' he said in a commanding voice.

Because we had already arrived in front of the church, we had no choice but to go back a few steps and started walking again towards him, pretending that we were just arriving to satisfy his purpose. It was very much like a wedding rehearsal exercise. In the process, I glanced at him from the corner of my eye and I could see his little finger busy flicking on the camera switch, creating a clicking sound which continued for a few seconds. One would have thought that a couple of photographs would be enough to meet his needs, but no. As if this series of photos he took outside were not enough, he followed us inside the church to take more pictures in different positions and places.

Standing a few feet near the back of the church, opposite some ladies, who were busy preparing refreshments for their guests, was the incumbent, Reverend Douglas Moore. He greeted us in the area which seemed to have been converted for refreshments and socialisation.

Facing the altar made me think of a wedding ceremony I took at the church some years ago. I thought to myself how good it was to revisit the church for this important prayer mission. Walking through those huge wooden doors reminded me very much of the 'Wedding March' and wedding party passing through all those years earlier.

The article and two of the many photographs taken at St Cuthbert's, which were published in the *Lancashire Evening Telegraph* are reproduced here with the paper's permission:

Walking in the Light of the Lord

Three clergymen are walking 105 miles across Lancashire to boost their power of prayer. The trio are stopping en route to pray in people's homes, outside schools and hospitals and even on a building site. The former Vicar of St Barnabas Church, Blackburn, Canon Herrick Daniel, the Bishop of Lancaster Rt Rev Geoff Pearson and assistant missioner of the Blackburn Diocese Rev Sam Corley set off from Silverdale on Sunday. Yesterday they visited St Luke's Church in Bank Top, and the Redeemer Church in Ewood, Blackburn, before making their way to St Cuthbert's Church, in Blackburn Road, and St Peter's Church, in Church Road, Darwen.

They will finish their walk in Fleetwood on Sunday, having travelled up to 18 miles a day to visit 43 churches.

Rev Corley, who came up with the idea of the 'prayer path', said: "So often you drive through areas en route to a church and you don't get to know the communities there.

"You learn so much more if you do it on foot. We are being joined every day by local parishioners and it encourages them to think about the way in which they pray.

"Most people think that you need to get down on your knees while clasping your hands and closing your eyes in order to pray but that is not so.

"We have been invited into homes where people are ill or going through a difficult time. We have stopped outside churches and hospitals, where we think people may benefit from having a prayer said for them.

"We have even prayed on a building site after the workers there mistook our fluorescent jackets for site jackets.

"They asked us if we were the joiners and we said 'no
we're reverends.' They were interested in what we were
doing."

The group chose comfy walking clothes over their usual
dog collars – although the Bishop does have his wooden
crook. Food and shelter are being offered by the communities they walk through. Rev Corley said, "We have had a very
warm welcome everywhere."

Our mission completed at St Cuthbert's, we moved on to St
Peter's Church which stands firmly on top of a hill at the pinnacle of
Darwen town centre. Climbing hills was yet again featuring consis-
tently on our journey.

When we arrived at St Peter's Church at 1.00 pm we were honoured to be served our meal by the Team Rector, Reverend Andrew
Holliday. Another thing that impressed me greatly at St Peter's
Church with St Paul, Hoddleson was the prominent way they
proudly displayed the Mission Action Plan prayer, filling the complete back of their magazine called *The Messenger*. (See 'Diocesan
Vision for Growth'.).

St Peter's Church doors have been opened for public worship
since 1829 when it was fully established, and this magnificent
building has become an important part of Darwen's architecture and
history. The church has been engaged in a massive improvement
project to modernise its existing facilities and to create new ones –
refurbishing the church in several areas, as well as coping with
regular expenses in maintaining its existing business.

The church body has a very ambitious vision of a purpose-built
community centre to facilitate various groups of all ages. The plan
is to create comfortable meeting rooms, new kitchen facilities, and
new car park areas. They do have a dedicated project group in opera-
tion to see both the existing and new projects through. This involves
constantly raising money, which they have been doing successfully;
their money-raising is likely to continue for some time to come,
as the total sum of the project is estimated to be in the region of
£1,500,000. I have been in this area of raising large amounts of
money in the church to fund big projects so I know exactly what

it feels like! That is why we were delighted to pray with them and wish them every blessing in their effort for this useful and far-reaching venture.

Geoff left us after a lovely lunch at St Peter's Church in Darwen town for a meeting at Bishopthorpe in York. Meanwhile, Sam and I proceeded to the town of Standish, a distance of twenty miles away. I couldn't help thinking of the trio who, due to circumstances beyond their control, had to be separated temporarily at Berea with the intention of rejoining each other soon, which was also our intention. We read from the biblical account: 'The brothers immediately sent Paul to the coast, but Silas and Timothy stayed at Berea. The men who escorted Paul brought him to Athens and then left with instructions for Silas and Timothy to join him as soon as possible' (Acts 17:14,15, NIV).

Sam and I arrived at St Wilfred's Church in Standish at 2.30 pm, half an hour earlier than originally planned, which in fact was a blessing because we had very little time to spare, as our next appointment was in Chorley at 4.30 pm. Due to our early arrival we had to wait outside for a little while until our host arrived. The curate, Reverend Suzy McCarter and the vicar, Reverend Michael Everitt soon arrived to welcome us. The news of Geoff's absence was regretfully conveyed to them. They were disappointed, but fully understood that his absence could not be avoided.

Within an hour, eight parishioners who had heard about our prayer visit came to meet us. They were all very friendly and shared life experiences and church matters with us beautifully. In addition, we received a warm greeting from four Australians who happened to visit St Wilfred's Church while we were there. They had come to carry out research, from the church's register book, into their family who had links with the parish church. At one point I was deeply engaged in conversation with them about the history of cricket in Australia. I am a cricketer myself and we discussed some of the famous cricketers that Australia had produced in the past history of the game, which brought a broad smile to their faces. However, we all sadly acknowledged that the present team were not so outstanding as their forerunners. Our sporty conversation suddenly ended when we were invited to go on a sightseeing tour in and around the church.

This thirteenth-century ancient church was probably the most beautiful we had seen up to this point in our journey through the diocese of Blackburn. It is said that this magnificent church was founded in the year AD 1205, which gives it 805 years of outstanding history. It has a profound effect on the community at large. As I walked inside the church, one of my first observations was a magnificent stained-glass window standing prominently inside this ancient building, and a few feet on the left was another one which could not escape my attention. It is something of sheer refinement and inspiration which is well worth seeing.

The church is deeply involved in the community life where it is situated. After praying in the chapel with the church officials and people, we were introduced to members of a bowling club a few hundred yards to the western side of the parish. We were fortunate to arrive at a time when the club members were engaged in a game of bowls. I actually counted twelve people on the green. There were a few spectators walking around who were very friendly. Some of them were very keen to enquire about our journey. I felt very privileged when a man approached me and said casually, 'Could you do me a favour?' I responded with another question, 'What is it?' He explained in a rather subdued voice that he had unfortunately trapped one of his fingers in a door, and he obviously believed that prayer would help. Without any further questioning, I prayed for his injured finger in faith that the good Lord would heal him.

With the serious session of prayer completed, we walked around the bowling green talking to people, and were offered refreshments which we welcomed. Mission completed, we said goodbye to the folks there, and I was pleasantly surprised when someone by the name of Brian handed over to me a beautiful ornament with the words, 'Here's something to remember us by at the bowling green.' I gladly accepted his generosity and said, 'Thank you!' On the way up from the bowling green to the main road near the church, I saw a peculiar shaped house. The unusual feature of the building compelled me to enquire about its history and characteristics. I understand that it is called Bramley Court, which was significantly, named after Michael's predecessor.

Walking around the charming township of Standish in Lancashire in the north-west of England was something I enjoyed tremendously, and I treasure the memory of it all. Standish is a spectacular township with a long and colourful history, with a population of only about 17,000. In its past history, it has enjoyed a rich industrial heritage of coal and cotton, and the monumental changes in the twentieth and twenty-first centuries have made a significant difference to its present-day life. It is good practice that the church is involved in some way or another in this thriving community with a diverse range of organisations, covering a wide range of subjects. It is good also that St Wilfred's Church is not bearing this load alone. I understand that it is presently sharing together with St Marie's Church and Standish Methodist Church together in a covenant of unity.

As planned, we made it to St George's Church in Chorley at 4.30 pm to be welcomed by the incumbent, Reverend Tim Wilby. He was delighted to see us, and showed us round this gigantic church. St George's Church, which is proudly standing in the centre of Chorley town, with a tower 100 feet high, is undoubtedly the biggest one, and possibly the most capacious parish church in the whole of the diocese of Blackburn. The brain behind the design of this beautiful building is that of Thomas Rickman, probably one of the greatest architects of his time. The church was designed to hold 2,000 people comfortably, including the 800 capacity on the floor upstairs. It has a striking, colourful window which I understand is known as 'The Stained Glass Collage'.

From what I understand, two major events in past history have had enormous effect in the church building and the parish as a whole, namely the Industrial Revolution and the Napoleonic wars, to which it owes the success of its existence. The cotton industry was first introduced to the town of Chorley in 1660, which in fact had been a market town since 1256. By 1790, Chorley saw the construction of spinning mills in the town as the population explosion inevitably began. As we walked through Chorley, it was evident that it is compact in terms of the careful arrangement of its streets, shops, amenities, offices and leisure facilities. In 1818, parliament set up a Church Building Commission with £1,000,000 in reparations from the defeated French.

It is interesting that St George's Church was built as a chapel of ease in 1825 within the parish of St Laurence's, and it was not until 1835 that district status was accredited to it. The reason behind it is quite clear. With the population explosion, it soon became plain that the main parish church of St Laurence's in Chorley, of which part of it dated right back to the thirteenth century, was inadequate with its facilities to cope with the fast-growing population. Therefore, in 1856 St George's Church in Chorley was created as a separate parish church altogether in this heavily populated area.

St George's, with its thriving and enthusiastic congregation, is fully engaged in the community with numerous church organisations and other community-related activities based in the church premises.

After praying in the upstairs balcony of this glorious church, we went across to St Laurence's, where Canon John Cree was the rector until recently. St Laurence's Church was elevated from the status of a chapel to the rectory of Croston to that of a parish in its own right in the year 1793.

I have some happy memories of St Laurence's Church, where I used to lecture in biblical exposition of the New Testament and other related subjects. I thoroughly enjoyed my time in the Bible college where it was based, when Canon John Cree was there. When John was vicar of Emmanuel Church in Blackburn, I shared my vision with him of a Christian Foundation College at St Barnabas Church and community centre, and he supported and encouraged me to proceed with it, as it was in its embryonic stage when I discussed it with him. So when he eventually moved to St Laurence's in Chorley he started a branch of his own based in the community section of St Laurence, and he invited me to be one of the lecturers. I was very glad to help. John and I got on extremely well and we keep in close touch on college matters at St Laurence's.

On the day we visited the church, I was no stranger to it and some of the people there. In fact, some of my former students from the college were engaged in making the refreshments for us. They were pleased to see me and I was delighted to see them once again.

From St Laurence's, we travelled to the Community Church in Great Green's Lane at Clayton Brook, still in the vicinity of Chorley, arriving at 6.00 pm. This was the eighth and final church we were visiting before the service to end the day at 7.30 pm. It had been a very long day, and it was definitely time for us to have a proper meal. I am pleased to say that it was provided for us admirably by the congregation of Clayton Brook. It was also a splendid opportunity

From the left: Rev. Herrick Daniel,
Rev. Sam Corley and Bishop Geoff Pearson
(Image courtesy of the Lancashire Evening Telegraph)

PRAYING AROUND

The prayer warriors setting off on their eight day prayer venture from outside St Johns church in Silverdale (p. 26).

Praying along the way: Views of Morecambe Bay from near Silverdale, the start of their walk.

Right: Reverand Stephen Jones outside Christ Church, Carnforth (p. 29).

Holy Trinity Church,
Bolton-Le-Sands
(p. 30).

The prayer walkers in consultation with the parishioners outside St Luke's church hall at Slyne Hest (p. 30).

A cheerful group outside St Thomas church in Garstang. The walkers are about to set off on their prayer mission (p. 34).

The prayer trio, joined by others at St John the Baptist in Broughton, look ahead to a long day across a muddy field to their next venture (p. 37).

This smiling group outside St Mary the Virgin church in Goosnargh has something good to smile about after a long and successful day of prayer (p. 38)

An enthusiastic group at the entrance of St. James' Christ the King church in Accrington didn't have to sing 'bring me sunshine'. The sun was already there (p. 57).

Inside St Cuthbert's church in Darwen.
Time to pray in the holy place (p. 57).
(Image courtesy of the Lancashire Evening Telegraph)

This is the way to do it. Canon Herrick Daniel joining hands with two other priests at St George's church, Chorley (p. 63).

The cross stands high over the prayer team at St Leonard's in Penwortham, accompanied by the Bishop of Blackburn and some parishioners (p. 69).

After prayer it was time to breathe the fresh air outside St Cuthbert's church in Lytham before moving on to our next destination (p. 74).

Enjoying the company of the residents at Fosbrooke House in Lytham, where the team dropped in for a chat, prayer and a cup of tea (p. 77).

Reminded of the hymn 'All Things Bright and Beautiful' (p. 36).

Map featuring the churches visited during the walk around Lancashire

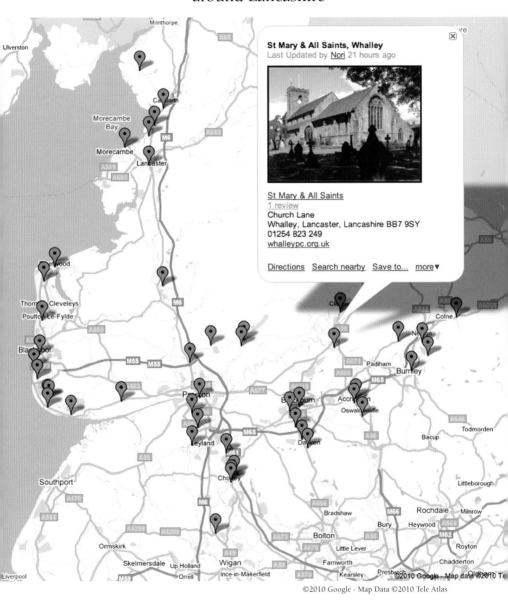

©2010 Google - Map Data ©2010 Tele Atlas

A Google map link is available on the Sovereign World website where you can click on the balloons to reveal details of each church visited: www.sovereignworld.com/news/100mileprayerwalkmap

for us to rest and stretch our legs whilst chatting to the people of the Community Church who gave us such a warm welcome.

The Community Church is located in the heart of a new housing estate. The development of the estate has necessitated the building of a church which is very modern and suitable to meet the demands of a vibrant community. It maintains an expression of kingdom life right across the area where it is situated. The church mission is to encourage people to enter into a growing relationship with the Lord Jesus Christ. The vision is to help their members to discover their gifts, talents and abilities, and to use them accordingly to fulfil their mandate in going into the world to proclaim the good news that Jesus is alive. This mandate is, of course, based on Matthew 28:16–20: 'Then the eleven disciples went to Galilee, to the mountain where Jesus had told them to go. When they saw him, they worshipped him; but some doubted. Then Jesus came to them and said, 'All authority in heaven and on earth has been given to me. Therefore go and make disciples of all nations, baptising them in the name of the Father and of the Son and of the Holy Spirit, and teaching them to obey everything I have commanded you. And surely I am with you always, to the very end of the age' (NIV).

After a delicious meal, we gathered into the Community Church for the evening service at 7.30 pm which the curate, Reverend Tom Donaghey, had organised. It was a well organised and inspiring service, with all the items surrounding the theme of pilgrimage. These included songs, psalms, readings, talks, prayers and interaction. It was a beautiful setting, with Taizé music led by their enthusiastic worship group. (Taizé music originates from the ecumenical Christian monastic order in Taizé, France.) The chairs in the church were set deliberately in the form of a cross and, in the absence of Geoff, who had gone to a meeting at the Archbishop of York's Palace, Sam and myself were called to take a prominent place in the middle of the church where hands were laid upon us and we were officially commissioned by the whole congregation. I was surprised to see so many people in attendance and enjoyed it immensely. It created a lasting impression on me personally. I could feel, and no doubt others could too, an awesome sense of God's presence in this specially designed and formulated service which was conducted with meaning and exceptional inspiration.

By the way, it is worth pointing out that Clayton Brook Community Church is a daughter church of the parish church of St John the Evangelist, where the Rt Reverend Alan Winstanley is the vicar. It was built at the time when the Reverend Eric Lacey was the vicar of St John's Church, and instituted the Reverend Dick Cartmel as curate in charge of the Community Church.

Sam and I had planned to sleep in the Community Church after the service on Thursday evening and to set off from there to travel to Leyland on Friday morning, but after careful thought and consideration we changed our minds and decided to drive back to our homes in Lancaster and set off from there to our next post.

During the journey back home and the evening I spent there, I reflected on the eight churches visited during the day. It was probably a record number of churches visited in comparison with previous days.

Chapter 10

DAY SIX
FRIDAY 29 MAY

Leyland
Farrington Moss
Penwortham
Preston
Freckleton

I will praise you, O LORD, with all my heart; I will tell of all your wonders.
(Psalm 9:1, NIV)

Geoff rejoined us to visit five churches in and around the Preston area, after his meeting in York the previous evening. I had been looking forward to this day with high hopes and expectations, for three main reasons. Firstly, because it was getting towards the end of the week, and as such I could feel that the end of the epic journey was in sight. Secondly, we were expecting one or two special visitors to accompany us on the walk. Thirdly, Preston as a whole has a fascinating history and I considered it an honour to walk on the soil where great pioneers have walked in the history of the famous town.

The name Preston originally derived from the Old English, meaning 'Priest Settlement'. This explains why Preston has been called the 'Priest Town'. Evidence shows that Preston has a very strong Christian history and tradition which has been practiced there for centuries. In fact, the very picture of the lamb engraved on the city shield is evidently a biblical image of Jesus Christ, and the same image that represents Saint Wilfrid, who was himself a seventh-century bishop, and recognised as the city patron saint who historically is linked to the establishment of the city.

Preston is located on the north bank of the River Ribble in the north-west of England. It was granted city status in the year 2002, and became England's fiftieth city, interestingly enough, in the fiftieth year of Queen Elizabeth II's reign. Inner Preston itself has a population of 335,000.

Credit has been given to the Saxons for the establishment of Preston and, walking in its township and the suburbs, Preston shows evidence of Roman activity in the area, especially in the form of Roman roads. However, the nineteenth century saw a great transformation in Preston from a small market town to an industrial one. It was one of only a few industrial towns in Lancashire to have a functioning corporation (Local Council) in 1835, and it became a County Borough under the Local Government Act of 1888.

Preston is well known or even famous for Preston North End FC, which was the first team to be crowned English Football Champions. Preston was also the home of the National Football Museum until 30 April 2010, following the decision to relocate the museum to Manchester.

I was taken on a tour of the museum by a group of Preston North End's enthusiastic supporters and loyal members of the club; and from what I saw with my own eyes, it looked very impressive indeed.

Our day began with a wonderful promise from the weather forecast centre that it would be sunny and warm all day, news which gladdened our hearts on the way to Leyland. We arrived at St John's Church, where Reverend Alistair McHaffie is the incumbent, at about 9.00 am.

St John's Church is situated at Earnshaw Bridge, Leyland, and is described as 'a church family rather than a church building'. The church vision and drive is to reach out to the community at large with the gospel message and love of God. This is made clear in their mission statement:

We believe God wants us to grow into an all-age Christian community, passionate about learning from Jesus. We will live for Him
as we rely on His Spirit to shape our lives in our homes, neighbour-
hood and work places.

It was an inspiration to see the number of group activities maintained in the vibrant church of over 100 members, catering for all
age groups. Above all, there is a feeling of liberation and explicit
demonstration of Christian love and fellowship which is expressed
in the words, 'At the heart of everything we do is the love and truth
of God made known to us in His Son, Jesus Christ, as the Bible is
taught and explained.'

In conclusion, it may be true to say that there is something interesting and exciting for men, women, young people and children at St
John's Church – all contributing to make it a living, growing church.

After sharing and praying with them, we left for Farrington Moss
to meet Reverend Peter Hallett, the incumbent of St Paul's Church.

We walked the two and a third miles at normal pace and arrived
at St Paul's at 11.30 am to find Martyn Halsall, editor of the diocesan
See magazine patiently waiting there to accompany us to our next
church in Penwortham, and beyond. Also waiting in the kitchen
area while preparing some refreshments for us were four ladies, and
within minutes a local news reporter arrived to take some photographs of us and to report the story of the walk.

After sharing and praying at St Paul's Church, accompanied by
Martyn Halsall, we moved on to Penwortham, a distance of three
miles away, which we made for 2.00 pm. There, we had the honour
of the Bishop of Blackburn, the Rt Reverend Nicholas Reade, joining
us for a seven-mile walk to Preston.

When I walked inside St Leonard's Church in Penwortham,
where the Reverend Nick Mansfield is the incumbent, one of
the first things that struck me was seeing the big cross in front of the
church. The church is very modern in its appearance, built in the
nineteenth century in the parish of St Mary's, Penwortham. I understand that the original building, affectionately known as the 'Tin
Church', was replaced by this new building about forty years ago.

The church is situated in the south-west of the city of Preston and
is a member of Churches Together in Penwortham, on occasions
taking part in ecumenical services and processions of witness.

As I walked around the church and talked to the people there, I could feel an atmosphere of love and friendliness. I found that it was quite exciting when I heard that for several years they have been going on 'away days' to think and plan the challenges of mission, which the Diocesan Mission Committee have encouraged. The church vision is 'To know, grow and share God's love', and this is anchored in their mission statement:

We are all God's children
At St Leonard's Penwortham
We believe this means we are called together
To respond to God's love in Jesus Christ by
Worshipping together in joy and prayer, growing in faith
Responding to the needs of others in the community
Opening ourselves to all who seek God
Rejoicing in the knowledge that God accepts us as we are.

As we turned our backs to proceed to our next project, I couldn't help noticing an inscription written on the church which reads:

In the faith of Jesus Christ and
for the extension of His Kingdom.
This Foundation Stone was laid by
The Revd Canon R.G. Rawstone
on the 21st September 1969.

Walking on foot from Penwortham to Preston town gave me an ideal opportunity to see with my own eyes how the River Ribble divides Preston into two parts. The town is situated on a hill above the river, and on the main routes, north, south, east and west. It is surrounded by breathtaking countryside, the Ribble Valley and magnificent hills. At the bottom of the hill is a bridge over the River Ribble, south of Walton-Le-Dale.

I was fortunate enough to walk alongside one of the local ladies from St Leonard's Church who had a wide knowledge of the geography and history of the Preston area, particularly the historical association of the church and the town, where religious and trade processions had taken place since 1179. A celebration of the Guild Merchant, which has taken place every twenty years to mark the occasion, attracts millions of visitors.

The University of Central Lancashire, which is based in the centre of the town, has in recent years been an important feature of Preston, with 15,000 students. As I approached the town centre it brought happy memories to me, because I received two of my three degrees from there.

It was very pleasing to have quite a good number of people from St Leonard's Church accompanying us to the Minster in Preston, where Reverend Timothy Lipscomb is the incumbent. We arrived at 4.00 pm under the blistering sun.

The Minster is located in Church Street, in a prominent position to carry out its mission to the town centre and beyond. In its past history it has played a significant part in linking the ecclesiastical ministry of the church and the civic life of the town, especially with the association of mayors and aldermen ceremonies.

After taking a number of photographs organised by our reporter Martyn Halsall, we shared and prayed with the people at the church and left for our next assignment. That was the moment when the group from St Leonard's Church, Penworth, returned back to their homes. The reporter, likewise, left, as did the Bishop of Blackburn, whose energy and determination saw him through 6.8 miles to Preston. But for Geoff, Sam and myself there was still more work to do before returning to our homes. We headed toward Freckleton, arriving at Holy Trinity Church at around 7.00 pm, where Reverend Jim Percival is the priest in charge.

The village of Freckleton is located in the Fylde district, north of the River Ribble. History shows that it is one of the oldest villages of the Fylde. At one time it used to be a seaport with a boatbuilding and sailmaking industry, but now the main employers are BEA and BNF, with agriculture as a secondary industry.

It is in the centre of this attractive village that the foundation stone of Holy Trinity was firmly laid in 1837 by Hugh Hornby – during the first year of Queen Victoria's reign. The building was completed on 13 June 1838, followed by its consecration by the Bishop of Chester, Rt Reverend Dr John Sumner.

The church authority states that their mission at Holy Trinity is to worship God and to work in partnership with other Christians in the power of the Holy Spirit to fulfil their ambition in three areas:

a) To develop the spiritual life of all Christian people
b) To share the good news of the kingdom of God
c) To bear witness to His love and forgiveness

To fulfil this mission in practical terms, the church set aside the month of November 2009 to pray for eleven streets in the Freckleton area as part of their united mission with the Methodist Church.

After sharing and taking part in the last service of the day, which commenced at 7.30 pm, the three of us happily boarded the mini-bus back to Lancaster to our own homes, to prepare ourselves for the next day's adventure.

Chapter 11

DAY SEVEN
SATURDAY 30 MAY

Lytham
St Anne's on Sea
Heyhouses on Sea
Squires Gate
South Shore

We always thank God, the Father of our Lord Jesus Christ, when we pray for
you, because we have heard of your faith in Christ Jesus and of the love you
have for all the saints
(Colossians 1:3,4, NIV)

Up until last night we had already covered a distance of about nine-ty miles on our prayer walk, which was quite an achievement in itself, but as we came to the end of the week we realised that the road-show must carry on to completion. We planned to visit five churches in two towns, one city, and two villages to round up the week.

Throughout the week, Sam has been picking me up from my house between 7.00 and 8.00 am, but circumstances forced a change of plan today. Sam made arrangements with me the night before that he would pass by my house for me to follow him to the garage from where the minibus was hired. As arranged, I followed him in my car to the depot, where he delivered the bus safely. We then went straight to his home to pick up his own car to travel to Kirkham, while I left mine there for the day. We left his home in Galgate at about 8.00 am to pick Geoff up.

We arrived at St Cuthbert's Church on Church Road, Lytham, at approximately 9.00 am, where Canon Andrew Clitherow is the incumbent. The church is named after St Cuthbert of Lindisfarne, a devoted Anglo-Saxon monk and bishop in the see of Northumbria, and patron saint of the said kingdom.

One of the things I found striking at St Cuthbert's is summarised in seven words: 'Open hearts, Open minds, Open for prayer.' This supposition is expressed more fully in their mission statement:

> We the people of the Parish Church of St Cuthbert aim to embrace God's love, to share it in worship and fellowship and to proclaim it in the community.

To help with the proclamation of this good news of God's love, they have a trained pastoral care team offering Christian friendship to people in the community and beyond.

After sharing and praying at St Cuthbert's, we walked to St Anne's on Sea in Kirkham. Walking from Lytham to Kirkham was quite a moving experience for me. I discovered that Lytham is the oldest town of the Fylde coast seaside resorts. It is amazingly recorded in the Doomsday Book 1086, where the spelling of the name is 'Lidum', which eventually changed to Lytham.

In 1856, a railway line was opened there which made the town more accessible to visitors, and as a result it developed rapidly from a village into a beautiful seaside resort. In spite of the commercial growth, it may be true to say that Lytham retains a splendid charm and character of its own. As I walked along, I could see lovely houses, hotels, churches, shops and schools.

Our next stop was St Thomas' Church on St Thomas' Road, in St Anne's on Sea in Kirkham, where Reverend Peter Law Jones serves. St Anne's is a relatively new town in comparison with Lytham. I understand that it was built to accommodate the new and up-to-date fashion of seaside holiday resorts, and is located on the western side of the parish. The first proudly standing stone was laid by John Clifton, the squire of Lytham, on 31 March 1875.

This is the place where St Thomas' Church is situated to fulfil the goals set by the diocesan synod of 1993. The people there acknowledged that they are sincerely working hard toward that goal. Above all, they are continually looking for openings and ways to serve the people of God in the community.

As we had done so many times before in parishes visited, it was a delight to share and pray with the people there before moving on to St Anne's Church on St Anne's Road East at Heyhouses on Sea in Kirkham. When we arrived there we found that a wedding was taking place, so it gave us the opportunity to pray in the grounds, and to eat lunch before entering the church.

St Anne's Church was commissioned by Lady Clifton in the early 1870s, and from what I understand the precise date of its consecration was in 1873. She named it in memory of her aunt Anne. Originally it was built as a chapel of ease to St Cuthbert's Parish Church in Lytham, for the benefit of farm labourers and fishermen of the hamlet of Heyhouses, who had to walk for several hours on a Sunday morning to get there.

The church administration stipulates that the purpose of its existence is to love and worship God, and to make His love known to others in the community at large. They acknowledge that every Christian church should be a centre for healing through Jesus Christ, who is capable of meeting all of our needs, including St Anne's.

A striking feature of interest displayed at St Anne's is a heritage mural; a big tapestry which was embroidered by the church Broiderers Guild in the 1990s, showing places and events of significance in the history of the church and St Anne's on Sea.

Kirkham is a comparatively small town, which I suspect is the suburban area of the Fylde district, and it dates back to before the times of William the Conqueror. It stands about three miles north of the Naze Point of the Ribble, near the Preston and Wyre railway. The town comprises a variety of well-built houses and dotted streets. Kirkham used to be in the archdeaconry of Richmond in Chester diocese, but is now in the diocese of Blackburn, and that is the reason we happened to pay a visit to the parish.

From there we proceeded to St Mary's Church on Stonycroft Avenue at Squires Gate, where Reverend Graham Rouse ministers. The church is modern and is serving a great purpose in the area, and carrying out its mission into the heart of the needy community of Squires Gate.

Squires Gate is located on the south side of the town near the boundary of St Anne's and Lytham. It is regarded as a district within the town of Blackpool on the Fylde coast of the County of Lancashire.

This explains why the international airport of Blackpool is located at Squires Gate. It also contains a small railway station in the south of Blackpool which leads to Preston. It has a popular holiday camp-site, which was originally used as a military base during the wars years of 1939–45, but has now been significantly updated to suit modern life.

Fosbrooke House for retired clergy

We were highly privileged in the opportunity to visit Fosbrooke house, a beautiful home for retired clergy and other eligible lay work-ers. No prior arrangements were made for the visit, but by chance we happened to be nearby on the prayer route. So, moved by what some people would call an 'instinct of compassion', whereas others would say 'driven by the wind of the Holy Spirit', we called in for an exploration of the people and the inner life of the home itself.

We were not disappointed at the cost of a few hundred additional steps from the original route. From entering the premises we were heartily welcomed by a member of the staff who did not hesitate to show us around, and introduced us to many people. I couldn't help noticing the name of H.L. Fosbrooke proudly displayed. He was the vicar of Lytham until 1944, and archdeacon of Lancaster. He had the vision and put it into practice by caring for retired clergy, and was instrumental in the development of the house.

Historically the building was the residential home of Thomas Baseley, known then as Riversleigh, and eventually owned by Mr Sadler who was an engineer at Lytham docks. It was purchased and converted to Fosbrooke in the 1950s, instrumented by the Pension Board Scheme. The Venerable H.L. Fosbrooke was initially chair-man for a short while, and was a member of the board.

After our briefing in the main entrance area, we were taken on a guided tour of the building. One of our first stops was the chapel, where regular services take place for those wishing to attend. Supported by several local parishes, the chapel offers a tremendous route to inner peace, calmness of mind, and relief from the stress of everyday living; it gives an opportunity for reflection on God the Father, Son and Holy Spirit. We were told that the services themselves are taken by various people appointed to do so on a rota basis, a process that seems to work extremely well. Because it is set apart for this purpose, whilst I stood inside it gazing at the cross, I could feel a sense of awe and wonder of God's majestic power.

Our next stop was the library, which is adjacent to the chapel. It contains a good selection of books, some of them donated for the use of the residents. The house consists of thirty-one functional flats on four floors, well equipped with a lounge, bedroom with en-suite, and kitchen facilities. Each flat has central heating and double glazing, affording extensive views of the surrounding areas. In addition, the residents have the benefit of communal facilities, with a spacious dining room located in a position that allows the enjoyment of the beautiful gardens. They have a selection of three main meals a day, with an excellent choice of menu. During our brief stay there we were served with lovely refreshments by pleasant and friendly people.

The scheme is run by a competent manager with an enthusiastic team of dedicated staff. It was very pleasing to see a demonstration of their love and care while we were there. Living in a house like Fosbrooke, residents do not have the time to be bored. There are various games, organised quizzes, talks and entertainment by outside speakers, as well as day trips to local attractions. For those who enjoy walking, there is direct access to beautiful gardens. A short distance away is the lovely beach of St Anne's – not forgetting the famous holiday resort of Blackpool. There is also a weekly market at Lytham, and other services within easy access for the residents.

During our visit, we talked with both staff and residents and they all attested to the high standard of care, love and concern provided at Fosbrooke's House. Its reputation is so good that there are waiting lists. One list is referred to as an 'active waiting list' for those who necessitate immediate accommodation, and the other list is for those whose requirements are less urgent.

Our final assignment for the day was in the heart of Blackpool. We were engaged in visiting four churches, and another five on the outskirts. I feel very excited to record my observation of what I saw in Blackpool after walking on its soil with Geoff and Sam for several hours on a hot, sunny day.

The town as we know it today originated from the name Le Pull, which means 'Stream Draining Mosston'. A kind of land peat dissolves and discolours the water, creating a pool of black water. In the fourteenth century, a small settlement called Pull was there which gives the name Blackpool. In 2009, I was visiting the Isle of Lewis in Scotland, where I had a preaching engagement. As I travelled around the island I saw bags and bags of land peat by the roadside. So having recently seen lots of peat, walking through Blackpool with the realisation of what the name meant brought it all alive to me.

The first mention of Blackpool is found in the register of Bispham parish church in connection with the baptism of a child belonging to a couple who were living on the bank of Blackpool. It has a long and fascinating history that continues to thrive in the county of Lancashire. No wonder it has been called 'the gateway into the country of Britain'.

Blackpool has been described as the 'Capital of Entertainment'. It is one of the biggest, and probably the most popular, seaside resorts in the whole of Europe. From my observation Blackpool offers everything a holiday-maker could possibly wish for. It is world famous for the following reasons and creations: The North Pier (1863), The Central Pier (1868), The South Pier (1893), Promenade (1870), Aquarium (1874), Winter Garden (1875), Illumination Lights (1879), Opera House (1889), Blackpool Tower (1894), Tower Ballroom (1894), Pleasure Beach (1910), the Amusement Park (1896), and Blackpool Zoo (1972).

It is not surprising that Blackpool attracts 16.8 million visitors every year. It has 3,500 hotels and guest houses, containing 120,000 holiday beds.

I am pleased to say that in the heart of this magnificent town we found the Holy Trinity Church in Dean Street, on the south shore, carrying out its ministry. The church was erected in 1836, the year before the ascension of Queen Victoria in 1837. The church is forward-looking, with great aims and objectives in reaching out to the wider community. I was very impressed with the prayerful way in which the congregation are developing the church programme. For example, they created a Think Tank cell group, who spend a considerable time praying and seeking God's guidance. As a result they came up with the following mission statement, and they insist that the whole church programme is centred round it:

> God is – love is
> Nurturing
> Shining and
> Closer than
> You think.

NURTURING – On our journey together through life we seek to learn more about God so He will help us to encourage each other, learn more about ourselves and to worship Him.
SHINING – God gave us a living hope through His Son Jesus. We want to offer hope and new life to our community in the South Shore, and in the world.
CLOSER THAN YOU THINK – God is love, is in you, and is in me. Even if you feel He is a million miles away, He is right next you and closer than you think.

The present incumbent, Reverend David O'Brien, gave us a warm welcome and explained that this is an exciting time in the life of the worshippers. The removal of the pews has created an open space where people can meet to socialise and take part in various activities. The laying of a carpet has added colour, warmth and beauty to the church premises.

After a delicious meal in the vicarage, we had our final service of the day there at 7.30 pm. It was an inspiring service led by the worship group, and we prayed at various points in the church, as well as sharing our experience of the day and the week with the members. The vicar then summarised the evening, said the final prayer and closed the service.

With the night drawing on, as the sleepy sun was slowly disappearing on the horizon, giving way to the rising moon inching its way up the sky, it was a clear indication that we must make our way to our homes.

Jean Pearson, the bishop's wife, came to pick up Geoff and myself at 9.00 pm. We both had preaching engagements in Lancaster the next day, being Sunday. But Sam had preaching commitments in a couple of churches in Blackpool, so he stayed behind and slept overnight at Reverend David O'Brien's. Meanwhile, Geoff and I said goodbye to the members, and made our way back to our homes, which was a pleasant journey.

Chapter 12

DAY EIGHT
SUNDAY 31 MAY

Blackpool
Bispham
Fleetwood
Blackburn

The grace of our Lord Jesus Christ be with you all. Amen.
(Revelation 22:21, NKJV)

Lord, make me an instrument of your peace.
Where there is hatred, let me sow love.
Where there is injury, pardon.
Where there is discord, unity.
Where there is doubt faith.
Where there is error truth.
Where there is despair, hope.
Where there is sadness, joy.
Where there is darkness, light.
O Divine Master, grant that I may not so much seek to be consoled as to console, to be understood, as to understand, to be loved, as to love.
For it is in giving that we receive, it is in pardoning that we are pardoned, it is in dying that we are born to eternal life.

Prayer of St Francis

The inspiring words of this beautiful prayer express the deep feelings I had inside as we came to the final day of our epic journey around the diocese of Blackburn. My heart overflowed with joy to see that all three of us, and others who joined us along the way, completed the journey safely.

Today being Sunday and the final day, I took the Eucharist Service at St James' Church, Shireshead, Geoff took a Confirmation Service and Sam was engaged in churches in Blackpool.

At 4.00 pm we all met at Blackburn Cathedral for the grand finale. Walking through the cathedral doors was like walking home to me, because during my thirty long years in Blackburn, the mother church had become like a second home to me. I was made an honorary canon in Blackburn Cathedral in 1998, for which I was extremely grateful to all those responsible in making the decision.

Since this was the last service of the week, in this magnificent church, officially known as Cathedral Church of Blackburn, St Mary the Virgin, it is important to give a short background history of the cathedral and its vision for the future.

The cathedral site, we learned, has been a sacred home to a church for over 1,000 years, and there is clear evidence of the first stone being laid there in the time of the Normans. The church was designed by a famous architect named John Palmer and was built in 1826. This was the year that a New York woman called Gertrude Ederle became the first woman in history to swim the channel from Cap Gris-Nez, France, to Deal on the Kent coast, which she did in fourteen hours and thirty-nine minutes. Interestingly enough, the cathedral was enlarged later on, in the year 1938. (The year that the famous Yorkshire cricketer, Len Hutton, broke the world record by scoring 364 runs, not out, in thirteen hours and seventeen minutes, when England beat Australia at the Oval by the unprecedented margin of an innings and 579 runs.)

With the creation of the Blackburn diocese in 1926 from the diocese of Manchester, the church which was called St Mary's was raised to cathedral status. Additions to the buildings were continually made; for example, the famous panes of coloured glass and an aluminium spire which was added on later.

The cathedral is situated in the heart of Blackburn town centre, and forms an important part of the community as a whole. It is regarded as the mother church in the whole of the diocese. It is open seven days and week welcoming visitors from both near and far. It operates a gift shop and runs a café, as well as hosting numerous concerts and other activities.

The cathedral is very strong in its music repertoire, which explains why it has several choirs. The cathedral vision for the future is to develop an ambitious building project which will transform its life and ministry, as well as that of Blackburn.

I was honoured and very pleased to have had my retirement service there, when the Archbishop of York, the Most Reverend Dr John Sentamu came to preach on that memorable occasion.

This was the glorious place Geoff, Sam and I came for the closing service of the week. The service was formal, as one would expect in the cathedral, with Sam delivering the final sermon. All in all it was good to say thank you to God for everything, and thank you to all who helped in a small or big way.

In conclusion

I want to end with a few words of Scripture about the messengers who were sent to Corinth from 2 Corinthians 8:16–24 'I thank God, who put into the heart of Titus the same concern I have for you. For Titus not only welcomed our appeal, but he is coming to you with much enthusiasm and on his own initiative. And we are sending along with him the brother who is praised by all the churches for his service to the gospel. What is more, he was chosen by the churches to accompany us as we carry the offering, which we administer in order to honour the Lord himself and to show our eagerness to help. We want to avoid any criticism of the way we administer this liberal gift. For we are taking pains to do what is right, not only in the eyes of the Lord but also in the eyes of men. In addition, we are sending with them our brother who has often proved to us in many ways that he is zealous, and now even more so because of his great confidence in you. As for Titus, he is my partner and fellow-worker among you; as for our brothers, they are representatives of the churches and an honour to Christ. Therefore show these men the proof of your love and the reason for our pride in you, so that the churches can see it' (NIV).

Chapter 13

THE IMPORTANCE OF PRAYER

O God our Heavenly Father, as we travel through the pathway of our spiritual walk with You, guide us in our journey on this earth as we share Your unbending love and encourage others into a fresh vision of communicating with You. Grant us your protection, guidance and power to fulfil our pilgrimage successfully, through Jesus Christ, our Lord and Saviour. Amen.

Have no anxiety about anything, but in everything by prayer and supplication with thanksgiving let your requests be made known to God.
(Philippians 4:6, RSV)

The book has shown so far the incredible eight days' prayer walk throughout the diocese of Blackburn, and our experience in sharing and praying with people in forty-four churches in forty-three towns, cities and villages. Since prayer was the main reason for this astonishing journey, this book would not be completed satisfactorily without explaining the meaning of prayer and outlining its significance.

Prayer is a channel of communication with God; what my former professor at Trinity College, Dr Jim Packer, called a 'talk back to God'. As at the time of the patriarchs, biblical verses show clearly that prayer is calling upon the name of the Lord, as can be seen from Genesis 4:26: 'At that time men began to call upon the name of the LORD' (RSV). An ideal example is found in Genesis 13:4: 'Abram called on the name of the LORD' (RSV). Prayer, in association with sacrifice, ascertained Abraham's desire with God's will.

Early history of the children of Israel revealed that prayer was mainly through intercession, which is noted in the prayers of Moses in Exodus 32:11–13, Numbers 11:11–15, Deuteronomy 20, Aaron in Numbers 6:22–27, and Solomon in 1 Kings 8:22–53. Also, prayer was very prominent in the ministry of the prophets. Later on, in the book of Psalms, prayer became more formal as well as spontaneous. Out of the seventy-our prayers in the book of Psalms, there are prayers for protection, repentance, praise, communion with God, healing, vindication and personal guidance.

Looking at the ultimate meaning of prayer in the New Testament, it must be said that prayer is the art of talking to God. This is clearly defined in certain areas of Jesus' teaching in the Gospels. For example, the call to pray persistently in Luke 18:1–8, and not to be discouraged. Basically, some of the parables revealed the true doctrine of prayer in terms of its importunity (see, for example, Matthew 7:7–11). There is a blending pattern in the method that Jesus offers in His prayer life and ministry, which reveals the Father's will. It is not surprising that the results of His prayers were so powerful and effective.

The Acts of the Apostles forms a glorious bridge between the Gospels and the epistles, with the insight of a deeper meaning of a prayer focus. So much so that it is true to say that the Early Church was born supremely from the seeds of prayer elements (Acts:1,2,4,9,20,21). Moreover, there is positive evidence of how the church leaders were inspired in prayer throughout the book of Acts (Acts 9: 40; Hebrews 13:18), and encouraged the followers of Christ to pray (1 Timothy 2:8; Acts 21:5).

There is a culmination of prayer and thanksgiving in the Pauline epistles. This is expressed profoundly in Paul's letter to the Ephesians: 'I do not cease to give thanks for you, remembering you in my prayers' (Ephesians 1:16). Again, in 1 Thessalonians 1:2: 'We give thanks to God always for you all, constantly mentioning you in our prayers' (RSV). Of course, these words came from the mind and heart of a man who himself received answers to his own desperate prayer, and experienced Christ's presence in a special way: 'And the Lord said to him (Ananias), "Rise and go to the street called Straight, and inquire in the house of Judas for a man of Tarsus named Saul; for behold, he is praying, and he has seen a man named Ananias come in and lay his hands on him so that he might regain his sight' (Acts 9:11,12, RSV).

It follows that the heart of biblical interpretation of prayer is the remarkable truth that God, with listening ears, wants to be equally generous in answering the prayers of those who ask and desire answers from their searching hearts, which in this case led to a dramatic conversion. The prayer may have been brief, but it was profound. Having received such a vivid answer to my prayer on the memorable night of my conversion, I am convinced without any shadow of doubt that God answers prayer. It was at a Billy Graham event at Wembley stadium in 1966 that I arrived there to find the venue completely full. I tried prayer, and soon after found one seat available in the choir! These events led to my conversion and, as a consequence a complete change in my life.

In Matthew 7:7,8 some wonderful promises of help and blessing are made by our Lord Jesus, where He said: 'Ask, and it will be given you; seek, and you will find; knock, and it will be opened to you. For every one who asks receives, and he who seeks finds, and to him who knocks it will be opened' (RSV). These strong words of Jesus clearly signify that the living God has made provision abundantly to grant every holy wish of His children. There are three words that stand out prominently for me in this inspired text: 'Ask', 'Seek', 'Knock'. It is significant that on all three counts the answer is conclusive: 'You shall receive.' In fact, the book of James, which offers some practical advice on prayer, says, 'You do not have, because you do not ask God' (James 4:2, NIV). These challenging words of James lead to the question, 'What is the relevance of prayer?' The simple answer to this question is that God in His power demands it. He said to Jeremiah in relation to restoration, 'Thus says the LORD who made the earth, the LORD who formed it to establish it – the LORD is his name. Call to me and I will answer you, and will tell you great and hidden things which you have not known' (Jeremiah 33:2,3, RSV).

These positive words of the Scripture qualify the relevance of prayer, that God is ready to release immeasurable blessing upon us if we ask. This explains why the whole life of Jesus was crowned with the life of prayer. On one occasion, Dr Luke recorded that Jesus spent a complete night in prayer on the Mount of Olives. Jesus did not only practise the habit of private prayer, but He also taught about prayer extensively in His public ministry. In Luke 11:1–4 we learn that Jesus was praying in a certain place when one of the disciples approached Him with a special request to teach them the technique of prayer. Jesus made no hesitation in obliging him. 'When you pray, say: "Father, hallowed be thy name. Thy kingdom come. Give us each day our daily bread; and forgive us our sins, for we ourselves forgive every one who is indebted to us; and lead us not into temptation.'

I am impressed by the structure and content of the Lord's Prayer, which has a strong hold on humankind. It is a prayer model that is repeated both in private devotion and in public places; it is noticeable that people may disagree on many points of doctrine, but are united – or rather, linked – by the common use of this profound prayer.

During our prayer walk, it was quite an experience to discover the different ways that people pray in various positions and for different reasons. It was interesting also to note that some people pray when they feel like it; others say repeated sequences of words; some say memorised prayer; others, extemporary prayers; some don't pray at all; others, when they need something, and others when they are asked to pray. Because I believe that prayer is so important, it doesn't matter when, how or why a person may pray, it is never wasted, as God hears every prayer uttered before His throne of grace.

We know from experience and from the Scriptures that it is virtually impossible to grow spiritually strong without regularly communicating with God. Prayer draws us closer to the living God and brings us into an intimate relationship with the Lord Jesus Christ. A dedicated and deep, sincere life of prayer has unlimited power. Paul rightly states: 'For this reason I bow my knees before the Father … that according to the riches of his glory he may grant you to be strengthened with might through his Spirit in the inner man, and that Christ may dwell in your hearts through faith; that you, being rooted and grounded in love, may have power to comprehend with all the saints what is the breadth and length and height and depth, and to know the love of Christ which surpasses knowledge, that you may be filled with all the fulness of God' (Ephesians 3:14–19, RSV).

Such depth of power depends mainly on taking prayer seriously and acting on it, and reading and taking God's Word to heart and acting practically upon it. This lays sound Christian foundations from which we can build pillars of Christian maturity. This in turn will promote spiritual development and will give us a high sense of expectation to hear the voice of God more powerfully in order to encourage and maintain our Christian faith.

The Christian ears that are trained to recognise the voice of God will have no doubt whatsoever when the Lord speaks that it is the voice of divine authority. Jesus said in John 10:3,4 ' ... the sheep hear his voice, and he calls his own sheep by name and leads them out. When he has brought out all his own, he goes before them, and the sheep follow him, for they know his voice' (RSV). It is true to say that when we hear the voice of God clearly in response to prayer, we will then know what His will is. How often have we heard people say in perplexity, or ask, 'How do I know what the will of God is?' The truth of the matter is that God, in His mercy, is more willing and ready to reveal His will to His children that He loves so dearly than His children are ready to ask in prayer. God's desire is to lead and guide His people into the pathway of a victorious life. In seeking for the will of God, it is vital to distinguish between the doctrinal terms 'directive will' and 'permissive will'. 'Directive will' refers to His highest and most gracious purpose, whereas 'permissive will' is with reference to that which He may allow for reasons known to Himself – though not necessarily approve. In other words, He may even permit what He may not actually desire. However, when we rightly choose what is the will of God for our life it brings us tremendous pleasure, blessing and satisfaction. A leper cried out, 'Lord, if you will, you can make me clean.' Jesus, in responding to the cry of this man, stretched out his hand and touched him immediately, saying, 'I will; be clean' (Matthew 8:1–3, RSV). The result was astonishing; the man was healed of his leprosy instantly.

It is not without good reason that the psalmist pleaded with God to 'Teach me to do thy will, for thou art my God! Let thy good spirit lead me on a level path' (Psalm 143:10, RSV). The writer's deep desire was to know the will of God. The late Dr Campbell Morgan made reference in his book *God's Perfect Will* (Eugene, OR: Wipf & Stock Publishers, 2004) to the common use of the phrase 'to know the will of God', amongst Christians. The preacher in the book of Proverbs declared: 'in all your ways acknowledge him, and he will make straight your paths' and 'Commit your work to the LORD, and your plans will be established' (Proverbs 3:6; 16:3, RSV). It is therefore important for every Christian to be certain of what God's will is for their life. There are several ways of measuring God's will. One of the ways is that if it is God's will whatever the circumstances, it will harmonise with God's Word. The Holy Spirit will also prompt and guide Christians to what God's will is.

Jesus wisely prayed in the garden of Gethsemane these striking words: 'And going a little farther, he fell on the ground and prayed that, if it were possible, the hour might pass from him. And he said, "Abba, Father, all things are possible to thee; remove this cup from me; yet not what I will, but what thou wilt"' (Mark 14:35,36, RSV). It is always wiser to allow the will of God to prevail in all circumstances.

Prayer brings us closer to God and opens doors to receive God's promises which are absolutely breathtaking. In Psalm 37:4 we read: 'Take delight in the LORD, and he will give you the desires of your heart' (RSV). This suggests that God will not withhold the request of our lips from us, because He has promised and He always fulfils His promises. Sometimes it seems too good to be true, but prayer seems to be the key that opens the windows of heaven for the blessings to fall upon us. Deuteronomy 28:1–14 are full of promises that God made to His ancient people but, similarly, apply to every one of us today. "And all these blessings shall come upon you and overtake you, if you obey the voice of the LORD your God. Blessed shall you be in the city, and blessed shall you be in the field. Blessed shall be the fruit of your body ... Blessed shall you be when you come in, and blessed shall you be when you go out ... the LORD will command the blessing upon you ... And the LORD will make you abound in prosperity ... the LORD will open to you his good treasury the heavens ... ' (RSV)

The same wealth of infinite treasures of blessing in the saints' prayers is recorded in Revelation 5:12: '... saying with a loud voice, "Worthy is the Lamb who was slain, to receive power and wealth and wisdom and might and honour and glory and blessing!"' (RSV) which the four living creatures sealed with a sound 'Amen!' in verse 14; a word translated from the Greek language meaning 'So be it'. It is associated with the doxology in 1 Chronicles

16:36: "'... Blessed be the LORD, the God of Israel, from everlasting to everlasting!" Then all the people said "Amen!" ... ' (RSV) It is indeed an expression of certainty and affirmation of the acceptance of the words issued in a believer's prayer. 'Amen' is found 126 times in the New Testament, either directly or indirectly, which signifies a positive attitude to prayer.

The apostle Paul was fully aware of God's willingness to answer prayers when he wrote to the Christians in Ephesus: 'Now to him who by the power at work within us is able to do far more abundantly than all that we ask or think' (Ephesians 3: 20). Many people in the Bible and down the ages have accepted this divine invitation and have seen God work mighty miracles for them – like Elijah, who prayed fervently for fire to come from heaven, and God honoured his desire and sent the fire to consume his sacrifice at Mount Carmel (see 1 Kings 18:16–39). Moses prayed an identical prayer of faith which parted the Red Sea (see Exodus 14), and King Hezekiah similarly prayed in desperation after being threatened by the King of Assyria; once again the result of his prayer was spectacular (see 2 Kings 19).

The incredible story of George Müller's faith and prayer is well known all over the world, when he began his work for the orphans in Bristol, England in the year 1836; how he depended completely on God to supply the needs of the orphanage institution. He was not disappointed because he received millions of pounds to meet the needs of over 17,000 orphans at the time. Countless numbers of people have been inspired over the years by this man's deep faith and earnest prayers.

These are just a few examples of many answered prayers that I can give, yet some people claim from their experience that they don't always receive answers to their prayers. A careful examination reveals that all things are possible with God, if we ask in faith. The Gospel of Matthew stipulates clearly that we will receive anything we ask if we have the faith to believe that it is possible with God (21:22). Secondly, we must pray in accordance with the will of God (1 John 5: 14), a point that has been made absolutely clear in this chapter. We must place ourselves with confidence in His hands, with the realisation that He will hear our prayers according to His gracious will. Thirdly, many people do feel sadly disillusioned if they don't receive immediate answers to their prayer request, but it is always better to leave it to the One whose timing is perfect. The psalmist was conscious of this fact when he said: 'I waited patiently for the LORD; he inclined to me and heard my cry' (Psalm 40:1). It was Ruth Graham who once said that if God had answered all her prayers she would have married the wrong man. We all know what a wonderful couple Billy Graham and his lovely wife, Ruth, turned out to be. They have blessed and inspired so many people around the world, including myself. Lastly, we are instructed by the Scriptures to pray in the name of Jesus. John gives an indication that when we pray in the name of Jesus, the Father is glorified in the Son, which signifies the seal of approval. Samuel Chadwick expressed in his book, *The Path of Prayer* (London: Hodder & Stoughton, 1974) that when we pray in the name of Christ, our mind, desires and purpose become one with Christ, which means a lot more than merely ending a prayer in His name. It suggests a deep desire in our hearts to glorify His Son by asking the things that are pleasing to Him. As J. Wallace puts it in *In the Day of Thy Power*, published by CLC, prayer moves the hand which moves the world.

I once heard a true story of a man who angrily went to another man to complain that he had something against him and that he was here to tell him to his face. The man replied, 'Before you tell me, let us both pray to ask for God's blessing on the interview.' He agreed and prayed fervently with him. After the prayer session ended, they both rose from their knees and had been richly blessed together, and he said, 'Now I will thank you, my brother, to tell me what it is that you have against me.' 'Oh,' said the man, 'I really don't know what it is, as it is all gone, and I believe I was in the wrong.'

The Bible asserts that the living God speaks, and it seems to me that both men in the incident above listened to the voice of God. It is as if they adopted an attitude like Samuel who said: 'Speak, for your servant is listening' (1 Samuel 3:10, NIV). It is amazing what can happen when people pray with determination and direction. It has been said that every hunter who shoots always shoots at a target. Similarly, it is important for prayer to have a specific focus. Matthew 10:30 shows that God is so specific that He even counts the number of hairs on our heads.

Many of the outstanding heroes described in Hebrews chapter 11 were men and women of faith, who walked closely with God and communicated with Him regularly. (In fact, the psalmist prayed morning, noon and night, as observed from Psalm 55:16,17: 'As for me, I will call upon God, And the LORD shall save me. Evening and morning and at noon I will pray, and cry aloud, And He shall hear my voice' (NKJV) – the psalmist's demonstration of a real passion for prayer.) We are living in a fast-changing world, where modern technology is so advanced that many people depend totally on it rather than on the Creator, who gives the scientists and other inventors the wisdom and the knowledge to invent and create all these things in the first place. Sadly, they seem to rely heavily on facts rather than on faith.

By contrast, one of the heroes mentioned in Hebrews 11 was Abraham, a man of faith who put all his trust in God's promises to leave his native land and go to an unknown place where God would send him. He heard the voice of God and obeyed. This is what faith in action is all about; hearing the voice and acting upon it. As a result of his faith and action, God in His power promised to bless Abraham richly – what became known as the three-fold covenant, promised in Genesis 12:1–3. To make a great nation of him, to bless and make his name great, and through his seed all the nations on earth would be blessed. These promises incorporated a binding agreement between God and His faithful servant Abraham... Like Noah before him who, out of the simplicity of his faith and personal relationship with God, knew in his mind and heart that he could trust God wholeheartedly. The Scripture went further, to add: 'By faith Abraham, when he was tested, offered up Isaac, and he who had received the promises was ready to offer up his only son ... ' (Hebrews 11:17, RSV). What seems impossible for human beings is possible with God. For example, the promise made to Abraham and Sarah was fulfilled when they had a son in their old age, to continue the lineage of the seed of Abraham.

It is interesting that Paul, in his letter to the Christians in Rome, implies that the promise God made to Abraham is offered 'to those who share the faith of Abraham, for he is the father of us all' (Romans 4:16, RSV). This means the father of faith, as he has been called. This is what God wants to teach us, to accept His promises in every situation that may confront us.

The long distance prayer walk brought back memories of my pre-theological college training days. Every term we were bound by the college rules to observe three days of 'silence' when the college authority expected us, as ordinands training for the church ministry, to communicate with God in meditative prayer. This meant that during the three designated days, students were not allowed to talk to anybody except God. Some of us experienced some awkward moments at meal times when we wanted salt, water or other condiments to savour our food. The way round it was to motion with our hands in a similar fashion to sign language. For those who were not good at sign language the motion had to be made more than once with much patience, until the communication became clear. The object of the exercise was to train our ears to listen carefully to the voice of the living God speaking intently to us.

It is astonishing how, during that precious time, the mind can be developed into a state of spiritual alertness with a high sense of expectation to hear God speak in a special way. In my first term at my theological college, when I was first introduced to this spiritual exercise, I was wondering in what way God would speak during the three days' silence. Would I hear an audible voice as Moses did by the burning bush, or would it simply be an awareness of God's powerful presence with me in the room? Amazingly, I found it was much more than an awareness. God speaks direct to the conscience. If we expect God to speak, then our ears will be tuned to listen to what He has to say to us. Like the inspiring story of Philip and the Ethiopian, recorded in Acts 8:26–40, with 29 as a key verse: 'And the Spirit said to Philip, "Go up and join this chariot" (RSV), with the result in verse 39: 'And when they came up out of the water, the Spirit of the Lord caught up Philip; and the eunuch saw him no more, and went on his way rejoicing' (RSV).

The voice of God speaking to us in prayer is encouraging, as well as being informative and instructive. Sometimes God speaks through His Word as well. For example, He spoke to Daniel in chapter 9:1–3. Daniel's immediate response after hearing the voice of God was to pray and confess, which covered the next sixteen verses in the chapter. Very often we come across the phrase 'Thus saith the Lord' when He speaks to the prophets or others in the Bible.

I ought to emphasise not only the importance of hearing God speak to us, but also the importance of acting upon what He is saying. I mentioned in my introduction how God made it clear to me that He had called me to take part in this historic prayer walk.

Now that the walk is completed satisfactorily, I am glad that I was obedient to the voice of God. During that time we fervently prayed for many churches, schools, individuals and other institutions, claiming the promise Jesus made in Matthew 7:7 that those who ask will receive. Above all, we went, we saw and we prayed. Because we believe that God answers prayers.

That is why, to conclude this chapter, I want to draw from three elements with full biblical justification how the prayer journey was worthwhile.

The first is 'Praying with other people': I am pleased to recall three examples of how God's servants prayed with others. Firstly, the apostles prayed with a group of women at Jerusalem on their return from Mount Olivet (Acts 1:14). Secondly, Peter and John prayed with other Christians in Jerusalem after they were released from being temporarily held on the occasion of declaring the truth of Jesus' overriding power to heal a forty-year-old man (Acts 4:23–31). And, thirdly, when Peter was freed from a prison by an angel of the Lord he came to the house of Mary, where he joined other Christians there at a prayer meeting (Acts 12:1–17).

The second element is 'Praying for others': During the testing period that the apostle Peter was locked up in prison, he spent a considerable time praying for others. In fact, in Acts 12:5 we read, 'So Peter was kept in prison; but earnest prayer for him was made to God by the church' (RSV).

The third element is 'Praying in the Church': We have the supreme incidence in Luke 24:52,53,: when Jesus' mission on the earth was completed, He was taken up to heaven in full view of His disciples, who returned to the city of Jerusalem and entered the temple praising and blessing God in His house for all they had experienced (Luke 24:53).

Similarly, during our unforgettable prayer walk journey, we prayed with other people, with our eyes fixed on the Lord, who promised to hear the cry of His children. Secondly, we prayed for others with deep concern in our hearts that the God of grace would hear our prayer for them. Finally, we prayed inside over forty churches that the good Lord would meet their many needs; spiritually, financially, and in other ways.

Chapter 14

REFLECTION ON THE HUNDRED MILE PRAYER WALK

And now these three remain: faith, hope and love. But the greatest of these is love.
(1 Corinthians 13:13, NIV)

Christian love in action

By way of summary, I am pleased to reflect on three main elements we experienced extensively during our hundred mile prayer walk throughout the diocese of Blackburn. Namely: love, fellowship and hospitality.

For many years now I have been preaching and teaching on the concept of love, both inside and outside the Christian Church. The long distance prayer walk gave me a golden opportunity to give and receive Christian love in practical ways, inside and outside the Church. I don't mean a love that exists only in the mind – what the theologians called an 'intellectual love' – but a love that is practised positively in reality; the kind of love that compels us to take care of people whoever they are, and to show kindness to others without counting the cost. Jesus illustrates this beautifully in the story of the Good Samaritan found in Luke 10:30–37.

The New Testament writers consistently pointed to the cross of Jesus Christ as the crowning proof of the reality of God's love for us and, as such, we are under obligation to show our own love to other people (1 John 4:11). Love therefore becomes a two-way system, in receiving as well as in giving.

This kind of love in the Christian circle may be interpreted as 'compassion'. Jesus by definition called it a 'new commandment' (John 13:34,35, RSV). The question arises: Why call love 'new' when it had already been established as a commandment thousands of years ago in the Old Testament, for example in Leviticus 19:18: 'you shall love your neighbour as yourself' (RSV)? Having experienced it fully on our journey, I understand in reality that Jesus was talking about the practicality of love that manifests itself in action. A phrase that Barack Obama used repeatedly during his presidential campaign which strikes me forcefully in putting words into action was 'Talk the talk, but walk the walk'. No doubt other people before and after him have used the phrase extensively to mean put the words we preach into deeds.

I am happy to say that love was not only an experience on our pilgrimage, it was also a common language shared with others in practical terms. Very much in line with Reverend Henry Drummond's concept of visitors on the mission field, he expresses in his sermon, *The Greatest Thing in the World*, the thought that love is the only language that all nations can speak alike.

Recalling the life and work of David Livingstone, the famous English missionary who could not speak a word in the African language when he first went to visit them, he showed them real love in practical terms when he went into their homes, as well as sharing with them elsewhere on the mission field. They understood him and received him joyfully. Indeed, that is one of the reasons why Livingstone left the imprint of love on the pages of missionary history.

Before we embarked on the journey I couldn't help thinking of what kind of reception we would receive in the churches and homes to be visited. My anxiety quickly disappeared after the first few churches visited, because of the warm welcome and overwhelming love and kindness shown to us. This, in effect, gave me tremendous confidence to press on with the rest of the journey. I was discovering more and more as we travelled along that love was a relationship that was characterised by kindness positively and purposefully by the people of God in the churches, and supremely in the community at large. Individuals were making every effort to welcome us with open arms of love; some whom we knew and others whom we had never met before. Amazingly, we were witnessing 1 John 4:11,12 in action, which says: 'Beloved, if God so loved us, we also ought to love one another. No man has ever seen God; if we love one another, God abides in us and his love is perfected in us' (RSV).

Love in this case is an effect, and the supreme expression of God's love is essentially seen as a model for us to reflect upon in loving others. The ingredients of its production is given by the apostle Paul in 1 Corinthians 13, where he says that love is measured by the kindness that is shown to another person. I must admit that kindness as such was shown to us over and over again on the journey. It is therefore true to say that our brothers and sisters in Christ were fulfilling the condition of unselfishness mentioned by Paul – a point which is emphatic in Jesus' own teaching to love others as you love yourself.

I like the way that Reverend Drummond puts it when he once proclaimed in a sermon at All Souls Church, London: 'I shall pass through this world but once. Any good thing therefore that I can do, or any kindness that I can show to any human being, let me do it now. Let me not defer it or neglect it, for I shall not pass this way again.'

After conversing and sharing with people of different nationalities, professions and faiths, including men, women and children, I came to the conclusion that love, as described in extensive detail above, is the unifying force that all people have in common. Whatever creed, colour or language, it is the identifying mark of humanity. This explains why Reverend John Stott said that human beings who do not love other human beings have virtually ceased to be human, because part of the uniqueness of human beings made in the image of the living God, is their ability or capacity to love others. This is not surprising since the Bible states that God is love (1 John 4:16).

The apostle Paul went one step further to say: 'For this reason, because I have heard of your faith in the Lord Jesus and your love toward all the saints, I do not cease to give thanks for you, remembering you in my prayers' (Ephesians 1:15,16, RSV). Paul had the same concern for the Christians in Galatia when he wrote: ' ... but through love be servants of one another. For the whole law is fulfilled in one word, "You shall love your neighbour as yourself"' (Galatians 5:13,14, RSV). To those in Corinth he added: 'I say this not as a command, but to prove by the earnestness of others that your love also is genuine' (2 Corinthians 8:8, RSV). He concluded his acknowledgement of the love that the brethren in the Early Church showed to others in these strong words to those in Thessalonica: 'Remembering without ceasing your work of faith, and labour of love, and patience of hope in our Lord Jesus Christ, in the sight of God and our Father...' (1 Thessalonians 1:3 KJV) Paul, of course, was speaking from his experience of how he was well treated, and the great love that was shared with him and his companions when they arrived in Thessalonica to plant the first Christian church there around early summer of AD 50.

I very much identify with the apostle's acknowledgement of the practical love shown to him and his companions. During the eight days' travel, we received love in abundance from the people of God. It was very touching to observe how genuine the brothers and sisters were in demonstrating this love.

Everywhere we went, people were glad to see us. In most cases they were already there waiting for our arrival, with a high sense of expectation. The beautiful smiles on countless numbers of faces brought joy and happiness to my own heart. In some cases, people were dutifully waiting in a line to greet us like members of the royal family, which made us feel very special. Above all, they were all so eager to share their stories with us. Their action brought the words of Jesus alive: 'By this all men will know that you are my disciples, if you have love for one another' (John 13:35, RSV).

Chapter 15

THE JOY OF CHRISTIAN FELLOWSHIP

*The grace of the Lord Jesus Christ and the love of God and the fellowship of
the Holy Spirit be with you all.*
(2 Corinthians 13:14, RSV)

The importance of Christian fellowship is stressed significantly
by the apostle Paul in his letters to the Romans (6:5 ff), the
Philippians (1:7,8) and Philemon (1:7). To this trio may be added
1 John 1:3: 'we declare to you what we have seen and heard so that
you also may have fellowship with us; and truly our fellowship is
with the Father and with his Son Jesus Christ' (NRSV).

I wish to echo these words of John and Paul for the excellent
fellowship that I personally found during the eight days walk in
the diocese. It is necessary to give a comprehensive definition of
the word 'fellowship' in a Christian context. The Greek root word is
Koinonia, which means sharing, communion, relating, participating,
giving, relationship, unite to each other, friendship association and
partaking with others.

This elaborate definition shows how important fellowship is in
the Christian community. In fact, it may be true to say that in any
community where people meet or gather together, it is vital to have
understanding relationships.

I believe very strongly that when God in His wisdom created
human beings, He never intended them to be alone, but to share in
fellowship with others. There is something very special in sharing,
and genuine friendship that cannot be expressed in words, but can
only be understood by experience. Too often I hear people say to

me that they went to this or that church in their local community but, because there was no or not enough Christian fellowship, they did not continue to go there, despite the fact that the speaker gave a brilliant sermon.

A good example was a lady in my previous church in Blackburn who revealed to me why she decided to stay in our church and how happy she had been since she entered the doors. She explained that when she first moved to the area she didn't know anyone and, as a Christian, she went to one of the local churches for several weeks. To her surprise, nobody spoke to her and therefore she left and came to St Barnabas Church where she received a very warm welcome and true Christian fellowship. This lady was a teacher in a local school. She became an invaluable member and worker in the church, with tremendous gifts that she shared in the body.

Having heard and seen how much people value Christian fellowship, I was moved to create three different groups in the church to deal in this vital area. The first was a 'Welcoming Group' to make sure that everyone, especially strangers, were well looked after at the Sunday services before, during and after each service. Secondly, the 'Sharing Group' – this group was operating on a more general level, which including caring throughout the week. The third one was the 'Visiting Group'. This group was responsible for visiting the sick at home or in hospital, and if someone had missed church services for more than three Sundays, to go and find out the reasons and to see what could be done about it.

One of the many reasons that the Early Church grew so rapidly, according to history, was basically because they maintained a lively fellowship. The practical outworking of the *Koinonia* was demonstrated in homes, the temple, the synagogue and in the community as a whole. This explains why observers outside the Christian faith exclaimed, 'See how those Christians love one another!' The growth of the Church is captured in the words: 'And all who believed were together and had all things in common ... And day by day, attending the temple together and breaking bread in their homes, they partook of food with glad and generous hearts, praising God and having favour with all the people. And the Lord added to their number day by day those who were being saved' (Acts 2:44, 46,47, RSV).

These verses show how they had a mutual affection for each other. Above all, they were concerned about each other's needs, cared for one another, heartily embraced each other, were kind to one another, loved each other and sympathised with one another. This unity in Christ was demonstrated wholeheartedly in the *Koinonia*.

This is the objective of Christianity which is expressed in the believers' attitude to one another. And it is one of the reasons why I am devoting a whole chapter to the subject with the associated words of 'love' and 'hospitality'. It was a high privilege for me and my two colleagues to share in extensive fellowship in the churches visited. Everywhere we went, the people greeted us with words of welcome or appropriate Christian fellowship expressed in handshakes or hugs, or what Paul calls a 'holy kiss'.

I was deeply touched when men, women and children in some of the churches we visited accompanied us for quite a distance on our way to the next church. The intimate fellowship with them seemed to make our task easier and the journey more pleasant – like the group who accompanied us from Garstang alongside the canal on Bank Holiday Monday, with the sun shining beautifully on the day; we had great fun in fellowship and prayer on the way to Broughton and Goosnargh. This is one example of many who came in ones, twos, threes, and in groups. Paul himself was aware of the validity of Christian fellowship when he wrote: 'Your life in Christ makes you strong, and his love comforts you. You have fellowship with the Spirit, and you have kindness and compassion for one another. I urge you then to make me completely happy by having the same thoughts, sharing the same love, and being one in soul and mind' (Philippians 2:1,2 GNB).

Not only the people who accompanied us, but also those we met inside the churches, shared immeasurably with us as well. In some churches, our stay with them was inevitably short because of the limited time we had on our hands, taking into consideration the number of churches visited. Though short in some cases, however, the quality time spent in prayer, in the service, over refreshments and in general fellowship were considered very precious to them and highly valued by us. I am reminded very much of Acts 2:42: 'And they devoted themselves to the apostles' teaching and fellowship, to the breaking of bread and the prayers' (RSV).

Fellowship with other Christians is an obligation that should be exercised in every Christian community. Having benefited so richly from the fellowship that I received and shared with my two colleagues, as well as others, I would go so far as saying that fellowship is a Christian duty. The reason is because the Christian life was never meant to be lived in isolation. The Church of God is a family in which we are related as brothers and sisters in Christ, having fellowship in a kingdom in which we are fellow citizens where, according to the Scriptures, Christ is the Head and we are the members sharing the same faith under the banner of the living Lord.

It could well be this thought of the Christian family that moved Paul to say: 'and when they perceived the grace that was given to me, James and Cephas and John, who were reputed to be pillars, gave to me and Barnabas the right hand of fellowship, that we should go to the Gentiles and they to the circumcised' (Galatians 2:9, RSV).

On our walk, we discovered that some Christians were riding high with joy and jubilation for several reasons. Some of these are outlined as follows: There is joy in God Himself, who satisfies the longing and hungry soul with His goodness. There is great joy in the knowledge of forgiveness exemplified in the verse: 'If we confess our sins, he is faithful and just, and will forgive our sins and cleanse us from all unrighteousness' (1 John 1:9, RSV), which brings me to the verse that seals it for me: 'but if we walk in the light, as he is in the light, we have fellowship with one another, and the blood of Jesus his Son cleanses us from all sin' (1 John 1:7, RSV). There was joy in the wonderful experience in having fellowship with them.

In other cases, there was joy in seeing an increase in certain congregations, as well as joy in seeing the power of the Holy Spirit moving in certain areas. Joy in singing God's praises, and opportunities to pray together with individuals and teams in various churches. There was also the joy and gladness of preaching God's Word and sharing in midweek studies. Joy in witnessing people turning to the Lord Jesus Christ. In fact, Scripture declares that the gospel is glad tidings of great joy (Luke 2:10), and even the angels in heaven rejoice over one sinner who comes to Christ (Luke 15:10). We as the prayer walking team certainly shared and rejoiced with them. St Paul summarised it beautifully in the verse: 'If one member suffers, all suffer together; if one member is honoured, all rejoice together' (1 Corinthians 12:26, RSV).

There is also the great paradox of the apostle in 2 Corinthians 6:10: 'as sorrowful, yet always rejoicing' (RSV) The question arises, how do we redress the balance between joy and sorrow which Christians experience? From what we saw on the journey, and if we can sing with confidence in the 'Jubilate Deo' that we serve the Lord with gladness, we can also identify with Paul, that we serve the Lord with humility and with many tears.

Again, we saw some of these on our journey. For example, the sadness of having to part from some of those wonderful Christians that we met and were getting to know to the point of sharing the love of Jesus with them and praying with them – we felt like Paul who, after spending three long years at Ephesus, said goodbye to the Ephesian elders, as we read in Acts 20:36–38: 'And when he had spoken thus, he knelt down and prayed with them all. And they all wept and embraced Paul and kissed him, sorrowing most of all because of the word he had spoken, that they should see his face no more. And they brought him to the ship' (RSV).

Perhaps many of the readers of this book would have experienced sad moments in saying goodbye to friends and relatives, or even some acquaintances. There was also the sadness of sickness, pain and bereavement. We listened to what they had to say in each case, and showed much sympathy as well as praying with them. One lady shared with such deep emotion the suffering she was going through, it was almost unbearable – I had to fight back tears. I am reminded very much of Lazarus who found a place in the heart of Jesus to the extent that when Jesus stood beside his graveside, John 11:35 records: 'Jesus wept.' It was more than sympathy, but what is known as 'empathy.' This means to step into the other person's shoes and really feel for them.

There were times on the journey when we heard of repeated stories of financial hardship which moved us to pray deeply. At times like this we encouraged them to stand firm in believing in the God of grace who supplies all of our needs. Also to point out people, and for that matter churches, do go through times of trial and testing, but it is important not to give up. Like Paul's encouragement to the churches in Corinth, 'We want you to know, brethren, about the grace of God which has been shown in the churches of Macedonia, for in a severe test of affliction, their abundance of joy and their extreme poverty have overflowed in a wealth of liberality on their part' (2 Corinthians 8:1,2, RSV).

There was also the sadness of decreasing congregations which was rather worrying, as well as churches that have been closed down for various reasons, and the heartache that has been caused for those who have been connected to them in one way or another. It is in times like these that we are reminded of the Word of God: 'I walk before the LORD in the land of the living. I kept my faith, even when I said, "I am greatly afflicted"' (Psalm 116:9,10, RSV).

There were those who carried the heavy burden of mission and others who were longing to see a revival in their church and community. Here, then, are the sorrows of Christians who love God more than anything in the world and cannot bear the thought of seeing God's Word and love rejected.

In the face of all the joy, sorrow, tears and sadness, we stood alongside our brothers and sisters in the Lord to share, encourage and pray with them. Even during the short time we spent with them, our presence brought joy, comfort and reassurance that they were not alone in their struggle.

As we said goodbye to those loving and friendly Christians whom we had such marvellous fellowship with on our journey, I reflected on the tension between joy and sorrow which I witnessed they were experiencing. I came to the conclusion that we can all rejoice in the hope of the glory of God, with the knowledge that those who sow in tears will reap in joy. As the apostle Paul puts it: 'as sorrowful, yet always rejoicing; as poor, yet making many rich; as having nothing, and yet possessing everything' (2 Corinthians 6:10, RSV).

Secondly, it is good to know that the Lord Jesus Christ never promised an easy journey in the Christian life, but He promised us strength, power, His presence, and the gift of the Holy Spirit to supply all our necessities in both times of sorrow and times of joy. In reassuring us that we are not in the battle of life alone, He said ' ... lo, I am with you always, to the close of the age' (Matthew 28:20, RSV).

Lastly, I rejoiced in the measure of victory and prosperity that I saw in so many of the churches visited, which I found extremely comforting, despite the hardship and affliction that others were experiencing. Which leads me to say with Paul: 'Blessed be the God and Father of our Lord Jesus Christ, the Father of mercies and God of all comfort, who comforts us in all our affliction, so that we may be able to comfort those who are in any affliction, with the comfort with which we ourselves are comforted by God. For as we share abundantly in Christ's sufferings, so through Christ we share abundantly in comfort too' (2 Corinthians 1:3–5, RSV).

Chapter 16

CHURCH SCHOOLS AND HOSPITALITY

Schools

It was good to see that in many church schools in the diocese of Blackburn that there was a close relationship with churches in their local communities. Of course, it has been said that the schools are the jewels in the crown of the diocese. It must be pointed out that the churches in the diocese have an important mission to fulfil in the schools.

It is well known that the diocese of Blackburn still possesses a large number of church schools, which is a good thing, especially with the changing character of the schools in our modern society. We discovered that many parents who have children attending primary schools were themselves attending local churches in preparation for their children to find a place in the Church of England secondary schools. They believe that the spiritual and moral standards of the Church of England schools are higher and better than the other schools.

Serving others

Contribute to the needs of the saints, practise hospitality.
(Romans 12:13, RSV)

The need to care and show kindness to the travellers is emphasised throughout the Bible, and it is taken for granted that the Christian

Church will fulfil the responsibility for a caring ministry to others. It is in the light of showing hospitality to fellow believers that I want to assess my experience of the eight-day journey.

Everywhere we went during our travels was like a birthday party. All the churches had one thing in common – the provision of lots of delicious cakes and other varieties of food and drink served to us, which we thoroughly enjoyed; we were grateful to all the people who provided the food and the drink. The excellent presentation of the meals in each case convinced me beyond any shadow of doubt that adequate planning and preparation had gone into it. The practice of hospitality goes right back to the first book of the Bible, Genesis, where Abraham passed the test of showing hospitality to three visitors (Genesis 18:1–33). Abraham's generous heart moved him to say: 'My lord, if I have found favour in your sight, do not pass by your servant. Let a little water be brought, and wash your feet, and rest yourselves under the tree, while I fetch a morsel of bread, that you may refresh yourselves, and after that you may pass on – since you have come to your servant' (RSV). Abraham's eagerness to welcome the visitors and to feed them was important for his reputation, because in those ancient times a person's reputation was viewed regarding the degree of the hospitality shown to others. That is why the book of Hebrews, reflecting on this incident of Abraham after thousands of years, reminds us: 'Let brotherly love continue. Do not neglect to show hospitality to strangers, for thereby some have entertained angels unawares' (Hebrews 13:1,2, RSV).

The thought behind the verses suggests that where there is real love to others, it will produce tangible actions in showing kindness to strangers which, in fact, we experienced during our journey. From what I observed of Abraham's action, the three visitors were treated as special honoured guests, which shows the practical ways that God's servants can be obedient to the voice of the Scriptures in showing kindness to other people. Genesis 18:1–8 therefore suggests that the principle behind the entertainment of the three strangers was recognised as a sacred duty.

According to New Testament teaching, Jesus himself recognised that hospitality was essential in the mission field. For example, the instruction He gave to the twelve disciples in their mission project in Galilee, as well as the direction of the seventy in Judea: 'Whenever you enter a town and they receive you, eat what is set before you'

(Luke 10:8). The seventy returned with great joy to report to him about the success of the mission.

Above all, Jesus illustrated prominently the true nature of hospitality in the parable of the Good Samaritan found in the Gospel of Luke: 'And the next day he took out two denarii and gave them to the innkeeper, saying, "Take care of him; and whatever more you spend, I will repay you when I come back"' (Luke 10:35, RSV). The object of the story is to show that a Good Samaritan is someone who looks kindly on a needy person and meets their needs accordingly.

Comparatively speaking, we met many Good Samaritans during the course of our epic journey. Like the lady in Baxenden who couldn't bear to see me go out walking in the heavy rain and kindly gave me her waterproof trousers! Food and drink were also plentifully provided from all the churches. We often found that after we had eaten enough, usually there was plenty left over, so much so that the hosts on occasions would invite me to put some of the leftovers in my bag to carry with me on the journey; an invitation that I often welcomed with great satisfaction. I couldn't help thinking of the episode of the feeding of the 5,000; John 6:12,13 records: 'And when they had eaten their fill, he told his disciples, "Gather up the fragments left over, that nothing may be lost." So they gathered them up and filled twelve baskets with fragments from the five barley loaves, left by those who had eaten' (RSV). Also, at the end of each day, a main meal was provided for us somewhere between 6.00 and 7.00 pm, just before the final service of the day at the host church. That is in addition to all the cakes and biscuits consumed in between five to eight churches visited during the day. If I knew beforehand that all these celebratory meals awaited us in all the churches visited, I would have weighed myself before setting off on the first day and then on the last day to see how much weight I had put on. However, the long walk seems to have necessitated the extra food eaten, because I did not feel overweight at the end of the journey.

Another important area which had to be negotiated was when we found ourselves a long distance from home and it was late in the evening, with the realisation of continuing the walk early the next day. Where would we sleep? The Lord knew the answer to this vital question. On every occasion, God provided a Good Samaritan who offered us lodgings and, in each case, I found that it was like a five-star hotel, where we were well looked after with much care and attention.

It is not surprising, then, that through the centuries in the mission of God's service hospitality has been regarded as a virtue of great significance. For example, when the two angels visited Lot in Sodom, Lot's response was: "'My lords, turn aside, I pray you, to your servant's house and spend the night, and wash your feet; then you may rise up early and go on your way." ... he urged them strongly; so they turned aside to him and entered his house; and he made them a feast, and baked unleavened bread, and they ate' (Genesis 19:2,3, RSV).

There were occasions when people offered us rides in their cars; other people who were deeply concerned after we left their church that we follow the right road, and accompanied us for a fair distance, until they were completely satisfied that we were following the right track to the next venue. Such care and concern sometimes touched me deeply. In fact, I never realised that people were so kind and hospitable in the diocese until it was put to the test on the long walk.

On one occasion when we arrived in the Blackpool area under the blazing sun, someone advised us to be very careful not to get sunburnt. I was rather thankful for the advice, because I remember vividly when I went to visit St Lucia in the West Indies I came back to England with sunburn because I was rather careless. So when the advice was given in Blackpool, I took extra care. I see it as brotherly care and concern for God's servants, as we make every effort to bless and pray with God's people in various churches; therefore, it is important that we look after each other's interests and share genuine love; as Paul puts it: "Most important of all, continue to show deep love for each other ... Cheerfully share your home with others who need a meal or a place to stay' (1 Peter 4:8,9, NLT).

It is good to know that Jesus himself accepted hospitality when He walked on the earth. We read in Luke 7:36: 'One of the Pharisees asked him to eat with him, and he went into the Pharisee's house, and sat at table' (RSV). It is therefore right that we offer and we accept hospitality from our Christian friends, not with the motive of what we can get back in return, but to see it as a Christian duty. Looking back to the many homes and churches which offered us hospitality and accepted us so willingly, we were fully aware that it was an act of generosity in fulfilment of the commandment of the Lord.

Talking about hospitality, when we arrived in Burnley we were taken on a tour to see the deprivation situation for ourselves. After walking around for about half an hour, we came across a hairdresser's shop with a group of Muslim men. One of the brothers who was accompanying us on the walk round the town explained to the Asian man who was obviously in charge of the shop the object of our mission, and he immediately offered us hospitality; an act of generosity which touched me very deeply, as we were not expecting it from non-Christian people. After we left the shop, we all commented on how friendly these Asian men were.

This brings me to say a few words about the value of friendship. During our eight days on the roadshow, we made many friends. Some of them we had met before, and others we met for the first time on the walk. There is something special about friendship which, of course, exists at different levels. I do not wish to make it complicated with the highest level of friendship, but the one I mean in this case is friends that take delight in another person for whatever reason. It was George Eliot who once said that 'Friendship begins with liking or gratitude'. I like the way that George Washington put it: 'A slender acquaintance must convince every man that actions, not words, are the true criterion of the attachment of friends.' This is very much in line with James' theology to be doers of the Word of God.

Some of the good-hearted people we met and shared with on the way had such beautiful smiles on their faces when we arrived, which brought a heartfelt joy to our souls. Though the time spent with some of them was short because of the true friendship, one would have thought that we had known each other for years. Like someone put it: 'Friendship is love without his wings.' That is what friendship is all about, one that is sincere and based on the love of God.

Before embarking on the long walk, I was apprehensive about what we would encounter on the way. Having completed it satisfactorily with all the love, friendship, joy, hospitality, care and concern shown to us in such great measure, I am delighted to have taken part in the epic journey with lasting memories of what we experienced. Jesus was absolutely right when He said to the disciples: 'Therefore I tell you, do not be anxious about your life, what you shall eat, nor about your body, what you shall put on. For life is more than food, and the body more than clothing. Consider the ravens: they neither sow nor reap, they have neither storehouse not barn, and yet

God feeds them. Of how much more value are you than the birds!'
(Luke 12:22–24). These inspiring words proved to be true for us
on the walk, where we were satisfied that God met all our needs
and provided for us beyond our expectation. For this and His many
blessings we say thanks be to God for everything. Amen.

Chapter 17

DIOCESAN VISION FOR GROWTH

If finding the right Crostic letters to describe causes that would bring growth, then the intellectuals would have no problem in identifying the effect and productivity of it.

When I first heard the term 'MAP', which in effect means 'Mission Action Plan', I thought that whoever first penned something so meaningful must be very clever. I commented that it was a brilliant idea for several reasons:

First of all, we know that by definition MAP is a route-finding object to help plan a journey. The new phrase, 'growing up and growing out' was an upward and forward-looking pilgrimage which necessitates a framework for direction.

Secondly, the importance of prayer is stressed by a number of contributors on the committee monitoring MAP. To quote from an article 'A strategic framework for growth', one contributor states, 'Only when objectives are prayerfully identified can we develop the strategies and devise the plans which will enable us to move forward in God's will.'

To set the wheels in motion, the committee responsible for the orchestration of MAP rightly composed an inspiring prayer in seeking for God's guidance on the journey:

God of new beginnings
We pray that you will
Transform your Church
As you renew us by your love

Give us vision for the journey
That we may travel light
And live increasingly by faith

Inspire, enliven and empower us,
So that along the way
We may be sustained by the life of Christ
In ourselves
In one another
And in the world

Amen

When the strategic framework for growth was first sent out to all the churches in the diocese, they were encouraged to use this prayer model as a basis for all mission activities undertaken. Of course, it is to be acknowledged that prayer is the bedrock of the whole project, and if it is to be successful then prayer will need not only a new definition with reference to spiritual growth, but also to be put into practise on a regular basis. Yes, this is fair, and a good thing to say in fancy words, but churches need to be convinced of the intrinsic value of prayer to make it a priority on their busy programmes. To help with the order or priority on the church agenda, I quote from the framework of the diocesan Mission Action Plan. Ann Morisy in her book *Beyond the Good Samaritan* (Chapman 2003), has a challenging statement in responding to God, saying: 'Prayer is fundamental. I say this on the basis of observation. I am convinced that prayer makes a difference and I am bold enough to say that I can tell when a venture is being regularly prayed for. It brings clarity as well as a unity of purpose. Time needs to be taken for prayer, and someone needs to take responsibility for helping this to happen.'

Ann's point is fundamental, as we observe from Scripture that we are not to be anxious about anything, but to bring all our needs to God in prayer (Philippians 4:6). I have seen in reality the number of churches that are anxious about every matter that affects church life, ministry and financial implication. To a great extent it is right that the churches in question should be concerned about church affairs, but if we take Scripture at face value then we see that objectives will be met successfully if prayer is given top priority.

I have discovered over and over again that when the spiritual aspects are right and communication with God is healthy, then everything else falls into place. Even the finance seems to be multiplied, and all the needs are met fully. It is not without good reason that Jesus said: 'Ask, and it will be given you' (Matthew 7:7, RSV). Jesus amazingly qualified His statement with the assuring words that everyone who asks receives. This is good news to the ears, but sadly, how many people read these striking words over and over, but do not take them seriously enough to put them into practise?

That is where the Diocesan Vision for Prayer is helpful in encouraging churches and individuals to embark on a new venture of prayer. To help with initiating, as well as promoting, extensive prayer meetings, the diocesan services are there at churches' disposal, to give advice and direction as to how to put it into practise. The diocesan offices have made prayer the springboard for MAP and that is the fundamental reason why, since MAP was first initiated, extensive prayer events have already been held throughout the diocese of Blackburn.

Admittedly, when prayer events have been held in relation to the diocesan project, there has been evidence of fruitful results. It is always good news when blessings are experienced as a result of persistent prayer, which often prompts further prayer.

Thirdly, mission as the centre of the project has given the churches a focal point. History has shown that a church without any interest in mission is likely to run dry, and in some cases, even be in danger of being eradicated. That is why the diocesan MAP is geared to assist in this vital area of church ministry. Again, a team of facilitators are there waiting to give necessary advice. Above all, the diocesan organisations have adequate resources available to assist all those who need them. Churches are urged to make use of them.

MAP focuses on the institutionalised programme of mission and how it is understood in the parish as a whole. 'Fresh Expression' (a term used to describe modern activities in today's church) in relation to MAP has given a new definition to mission in reaching out to lost souls. Biblical expression recognises the need to encourage all Christians to be witnesses in missionary work on our doorsteps in the diocese and beyond. Also, the church is called to the task of instigating discipleship programmes and to proceed in the commission of Christ. Matthew 28:19,20 records Jesus' words: 'Go therefore and make disciples of all nations, baptizing them in the name of the Father and of the Son and of the Holy Spirit, teaching them to observe all that I have commanded you; and lo, I am with you always, to the close of the age' (RSV).

Growing in faith

In the Bishop of Blackburn, Rt Reverend Nicholas Reade's letter, 'Going for Growth 2', he asked a vital question: 'How can we work together under God to support and encourage God's mission in parishes?' He gave a clue in the statement, 'Parish MAPs remain at the centre of our growth strategy.' The question raises two aspects. One is for parishes to have enough or unlimited 'faith' in God to believe without any shadow of doubt that He will bring about the revolutionary 'growth' desired. The second is for parishes to believe that MAP is the process which can be used to achieve the end product. Perhaps it will help to clarify this point with a definition of faith and the process of growing in faith.

St Augustine is well known as one of the first biblical scholars to define faith in its entirety. He states in his treatise concerning the predestination of the saints that faith is 'thinking in prior to believing ... to believe is nothing other than to think with assent. For not all who think believe ... but all who believe think, and they think believing and believe thinking.' Up to this day, some churches in the East still define faith as 'assent'. This raises the question – does Augustine's definition still apply to individuals or churches in the West? Perhaps it is a good thought to ponder upon the two camps or degree of belief.

However, the sixteenth-century reformers stipulate that faith or belief had an intellectual content in the concept of justification by faith. But the doctrine of faith must be deduced from the Holy Scripture to apply in the vision for mission. The Gospel of John states clearly that those who believe in Jesus Christ have the right to be called children of God (1:12). Likewise, Paul said that those who believe in their hearts that God raised Jesus from the dead will be saved (Romans 10:9).

The parishes exist to proclaim this message, and MAP 1 and 2, 'Going for Growth', are vehicles to ride upon. In order for this to be done effectively, parishes have to recognise the need of growing in faith. When faith is stretched to the limit of 'growing up and growing out', then the differences will become more apparent in the parishes as a whole.

St Paul writes in Hebrews 11:1 that 'faith is the assurance of things hoped for, the conviction of things not seen' (RSV). In fact, the act of faith, whether active or passive, whether for endurance or for achievement, is the extraordinary thought underlying the whole of Hebrews chapter 11. As such, Paul sees faith as a commitment to the unknown. Likewise, the churches of the diocese of Blackburn must bring the contents of faith into the reality of a diocesan framework for growing in faith.

Meanwhile, individuals and churches are encouraged to allow the power of the Holy Spirit to transform the life of the local communities. In the Early Church, the Holy Spirit made a huge difference in transforming communities, and down the ages the Spirit has revolutionised the life and ministry of the mission church significantly. The good news is that the Holy Spirit is still actively moving in God's Church today. I like the way that the vision for transformation is enumerated in 'Going for growth 2': 'A missionary church is transformation. It exists for the transformation of the community that it serves, by the power of the gospel and through the Holy Spirit.'

The Holy Spirit is God's gift to the Church, and that is one of the many reasons that St Paul mentioned the production of both the gifts and the fruits of the Holy Spirit to the Corinthian and the Galatian churches. He rightly indicated that the gifts were for the edification of the Church, which simply means to build up the Church of God. This fits in with the diocesan framework of growing up.

To apply St Paul's perception of the Holy Spirit's role in growth to the Blackburn vision in 'Going for growth', it is wise to explore more into the availability of the power of the Holy Spirit. The limitless power has been moved within the grasp of the churches, and it is up to them to invest more in the Giver of this unlimited power to transform the face of the diocese.

The following biblical verses show how the Holy Spirit was promised in the Old Testament, confirmed in the gospel, and the promise fulfilled in Acts (Joel 2:28,29; John 15:26; Acts 2:1-4).

Chapter 18

CALL FOR ACTION

Awake up, my glory; awake, psaltery and harp. I myself will awake early.
(Psalm 57:8, KJV)

St Paul in his wisdom gave the Church in Rome a wake-up call in these challenging words: ' ... it is high time to awake out of sleep' (Romans 13:11, NKJV). Having observed the situation in some of the churches throughout the diocese of Blackburn for myself, I will devote this chapter to a call for action.

To call on the churches in Scripture to awake is to suggest that the churches have gone to sleep, which may be true of the churches in our own time.

Although we are living in an exciting time, especially when the Holy Spirit is moving powerfully in the lives of many individuals and in churches at large, with tremendous gifts and spiritual fruits on offer for its edification, yet the Church generally is facing daunting problems and does not know how to cope and deal with them. Here are some of them: human trafficking, scientific discoveries, community relationships, Christian assemblies and religious education in church schools and others being replaced by moral ethics, climate change issues, falling moral standards, families falling apart, increase in crime, racial discrimination, people who are hurt and wounded inside, social injustice, lawlessness, widespread persecution, drunkenness (like the days of Noah, Luke 17:26–30), underlying boredom, uncontrollable flames of greed and hate, an affluent society and the quest for materialism, the uncontrolled flame of the Internet when used wrongly, and powerful pressure from the media, especially with the new world of modern technology in their grasp. The Church finds itself in a society where there is scanty knowledge of sin, and either little or no perception of righteousness.

There is a general feeling amongst many people that things cannot go on like this. This raises the question, where will it all end, and what can the Church, which is the instrument representing God on the earth, do about it? Most people would agree that the desperate situation in the world needs to be dealt with effectively. Taking into consideration that the problems are not easy to solve, the question must be asked, how can the Church of Christ Jesus deal with them? Sir Winston Churchill once questioned whether 'our problems got beyond our control?' This may well be true in the case of the trend in modern society. Therefore, the Church needs to put its house in order and develop new strategies in line with scriptural justification to deal satisfactorily with these overwhelming problems.

So often the Church is motivated by fear and remains powerless to do anything. I believe that the time has come for the Church to take radical action before it is too late. The Church must not be afraid to take new initiatives in line with Scripture to meet the demands of the day. It must never entertain the thought that there is nothing that can be done. Unlike Jean-Paul Sartre, who wrote a book called *No Exit*, the truth of the Bible is that there is a way out. If we analyse the prophetic words of the Scriptures carefully, then we should not be surprised at the things that are happening in our generation. Jesus rightly talked about (in Luke 21:25,26) the distress and the perplexity of the nations upon the earth, which characterises our own generation.

For this reason, God has equipped His Church with powerful weapons to deal with every conceivable situation that exists in our society today. When I was a curate in St Mark's, Harlesden in north-west London, I led a young people's group in Bible study, prayer and other activities. One young lad took Christ seriously and was eventually filled with the Holy Spirit. Suddenly his life was transformed dramatically and he seemed to become a different person altogether. He called me one day and asked, 'What has happened to the power that God gave to His Church?' His question was obviously very challenging, as well as fundamental, and caused me to think about it for days, weeks, months and years.

After careful thought and consideration, I have come to the conclusion that the Church needs more of the overwhelming power of the Holy Spirit to deal effectively with the present-day situation. In His fullness and power, the Holy Spirit has been called the heartbeat of the Christian believer and, as such, we need to know more of His extraordinary power which flows as a living bloodline. If the Christian Church is to look through its windows at a corrupt society and subsequently open its doors for sinners to walk in to find a better life in the Lord Jesus Christ, then it needs to know more of the power, and indeed the character, of the Holy Spirit in order to function more powerfully.

So often on Pentecost Sunday in the Church of England, everything is geared around what happened on the Day of Pentecost as related in Acts 2, without the realisation that a new Pentecost is needed and that we should live practically in it now to be of good use to God and His people, suffering for whatever reasons in a derailed society.

As early as in the days of Samuel, we have evidence of the outworking of the Holy Spirit in the school of the prophets where the Holy Spirit was moving powerfully, and as history began to take its course, it showed that He was actively working in the life of David; then Joel 2:28,29 promised that He would be poured in great measure on subsequent generations.

Jesus confirmed this same promise and said that He would send the Holy Spirit on His believers (see John 14,15,16), which was indeed fulfilled on the Day of Pentecost in Acts 2. Following this explosion of the Holy Spirit, it is evident that He has been actively working in the lives of individuals and the Church as a whole.

Among the many good gifts that Jesus Christ promised to give His Church, the Holy Spirit is the greatest. The Scriptures make it quite clear that there are four attitudes people can take towards Him:

1. They can grieve Him (Ephesians 4:30).
2. They can resist Him (Acts 7:51).
3. They can quench Him (1 Thessalonians 5:19).
4. They can be filled with Him – which is what is recommended (Ephesians 5:18).

Actions needing to be taken

These are some of the actions that can be taken for the Christian Church to make a difference.

1. A radical reformation is needed with God's guidance, and as seems appropriate to suit the Church in its present situation.
2. At the moment, many Christians are feeling at a low ebb. New motivation is desperately needed. Perhaps new machineries should be initiated from central offices to deal appropriately with this hidden problem.
3. Strong spiritual leadership is vital. The Christian Church needs powerful leaders with spiritual insight, talents and energy and, above all, a strong voice with divine authority to speak out against anything that is wrong against God, His people and the content of the Scriptures in our society today.
4. The Church needs to be more open and honest in dealing with people.
5. The Christian Church ought to face up to its responsibility with boldness and without fear. Fear can be very destructive, so it needs to be overcome in the name of Jesus Christ. It is not without good reason that the Bible records: 'Men's hearts failing them for fear, and for looking after those things which are coming on the earth: for the powers of heaven shall be shaken' (Luke 21:26, KJV).
6. Restoration of backslidden Christians. Many Christians have sadly left the Church because of disillusionment. Something urgently needs to be done to bring them back.
7. The Christian Church needs to rediscover a fresh vision for prayer to reach the heart of God. Perhaps 2 Chronicles 7:14 could be used as a springboard.
8. The Church needs also to rediscover the value of fasting for spiritual dynamic. This is to deny the body of material food in order to appreciate more the spiritual food. From my experience, I have discovered that when prayer is backed by fasting, extraordinary things do happen.

9. The Church ought to see God being bigger than society; therefore, as such, there is no problem that He cannot solve. Paul puts it this way: 'I can do all things in him who strengthens me' (Philippians 4:13, RSV).

10. The Church must aim to become more heavenly and let go of self-centredness.

11. It is important for the Church to become more missionary focused, and to encourage its members to take more interest in mission and to support it extensively in three main areas: Prayerfully, morally and financially (Matthew 28:19,20).

12. The Bible made some wonderful promises which are available to the Christian Church. It must claim them in the name of Jesus Christ.

13. Perhaps one of the greatest needs in the life of the Christian Church today is revival. The Church needs to find out why revival tarries, and what could be done to speed it up. It must look at past revivals and see what instigated them, examine its own position and make preparation to go for a spiritual revolution in revival. For example: The 1859 revival in Ulster; 1904 in Wales; 1949 in the Hebrides. Recent revivals in distant lands, for example, the Congo. Present happenings in various churches around the world.

14. The Church needs to re-enter into a covenant relationship with God the Father, Son and Holy Spirit in renewal. Although many writers have written extensively on 'Renewal and Revival' in recent years, the Christian Church still needs to be reminded of the goldmine that is there waiting to be unearthed, for the Holy Spirit to bring a refreshing well of living water from the spring of God's fountain.

15. God is looking for people today who are willing to hear His voice and to be used as His prophetic voice to the nations. It is the Church's task to prepare, teach and help to create modern prophets to be God's representatives in the society of today, which is evidently falling away from God.

16. The Christian Church needs to understand the true meaning of love in the context of 1 Corinthians 13, and to become a living instrument of God's love, without reservation.

17. Finally, we must put on the whole armour of God, according to Ephesians 6, to be able to deal with the relentless attack of the prowling enemy.

QUESTIONS

I have set below some questions with relevant scriptural verses for those who would like to use this book as a study course in groups or individually.

1. What is the meaning of prayer?
   Helpful verses Ephesians 3:14–21; Hebrews 7:25; Mark 14:32–40.

2. Why is it necessary to pray?
   Ephesians 6:18,19; Matthew 9:35–38

3. Do you think that prayer is linked in any way with the elements of:
   Thanksgiving. See Philippians 4:6; 1 Thessalonians 5:18.
   Adoration. See John 4:23.
   Worship. See Psalm 99:2–5.
   Praise. See Acts 16:25; Psalm 47:6,7.

4. Do you think that Jesus assumed that all Christians are intercessors, or prayer is a gift exercised by some? Luke 11:1–4; Matthew 6:5–13

5. What do you think are the most effective ways of developing a successful prayer life (for example, a course on prayer, meditation, quiet time etc)? Psalm 49:1–3; Psalm 119:97–99; Joshua 1:5–9.

6. Do you think it is necessary to have a special technique when praying?
    Time: Psalm 55:16,17; Psalm 1:2; Psalm 42:2–5.
    Position (Sitting, kneeling, walking or lying down.): Psalm 95:6,7.
    Place: 2 Chronicles 6:26–27; Psalm 26:8; 1 Kings 8:30.

7. Do you think it matters whether or not it is:
    Liturgical: Isaiah 6; Deuteronomy 9:25–29.
    Formal: Matthew 21:12,13; Acts 22:17–21.
    Spontaneous: Acts 2:23–26; 6:5–7.

8. Do you believe that all prayers are answered? If not, what are the conditions attached to prayer? Psalm 34:15; Psalm 40:1; Matthew 21:22; Psalm 27:14; Isaiah 59:1,2; John 14:13,14.

9. What are the most practical ways in helping others to develop an effective prayer life? Luke 11:1; Acts 11:5-18.

10. Do you find that it is easy to say open or extemporary prayer? Examine the difficulties involved: Acts 16:25–34; Matthew 26:36–46.

11. Do you think that general intercession in the main body of the Church is enough? If not, what other additional elements should be injected into our prayer life? 1 Timothy 2:1–7; Romans 8:26,27.

12. It has been said that holding bitterness and resentment in our hearts towards other people can cause a blockage in the answers to prayers. Do you agree or disagree with this statement? See Matthew 6:14,15; 6:1–15.

13. What's the difference between praying in the spirit and saying a prayer with the natural mind? 1 Corinthians 14:13–19; Ephesians 6:18; Jude 20.

14. What level of prayer can revive spiritual dryness? 1 Thessalonians 5:17; Psalm 23.

15. When you are going through a wilderness experience and are feeling extremely low, do you pray, or do you ask others to intercede for you? 1 Thessalonians 5:25; Hebrews 7:22–25; Romans 8:26,27.

16. In 1 Thessalonians 5:17 we read 'pray without ceasing'. What do you think this means? Is it possible?

17. If you are engaged in prayer and the phone mobile rings, do you ignore or answer it? Do you think that there are reasons behind the distraction? Ephesians 6:10–20.

18. Do you pray for something just once and wait for the answers, or do you go on praying until the answer becom es apparent? Colossians 1:9; 1 Thessalonians 5:17.

19. To what degree do you think that our emotions or urgency affect the outcome of prayer answers? Psalm 28:2; 1 Thessalonians 3:10.

20. How much time to you think is necessary to spend in prayer on a daily basis? James 5:18; 1 Thessalonians 5:17.

21. Do you think that it is necessary to keep a prayer diary? Why? 1 Samuel 1:10–28.

22. What part do you think the Holy Spirit plays in our intercessory prayer? 1 Corinthians 14:12–22; Romans 8:26,27.

23. Do you think that the church today has neglected the quest for healing in its programme? James 5:12–20; John 4:43–54; John 5:1–18.

24. What can we take from the Bible that guides our approach in prayer for healing? The follow is a list of different healing needs within and outside the church:

- Spiritual
- Mental
- Emotional
- Physical
- Healing of relationships

In reaching the end of this prayer adventure may I ask you to examine 2 Chronicles 7:14 and discuss. Once you have gone through these questions I recommend you read again chapter 18: Call to Action.

THE HUNDRED MILE WALK ITINERARY

Sunday 24 May – Sunday 31 May 2009

Day	Place	Possible Churches	Notes	Distance
Sun	Silverdale	St John's	Start of Walk	6.4 miles
	Carnforth	Christ Church		1.1 miles
	Bolton-Le-Sands	Holy Trinity		1.9 miles
	Slyne with Hest	St Luke		3.1 miles
	Morecambe	Holy Trinity,		4.2 miles
	Lancaster	The Priory	End day here	**16.7 miles**
Mon	Garstang	St Thomas	Start day here	7.1 miles
	Broughton	St John's		3.0 miles
	Goosnargh	St Mary's		3.9 miles
	Longridge	St Lawrence with St Paul	End day here	**14 miles**
Tues	Clitheroe	St James	Start day here	4.1 miles
	Whalley	St Mary's & All Saints		8.1 miles
	Fence	St Anne's		2.0 miles
	Nelson	St Paul's Little Marsden		5.7 miles
	Colne	Christ Church	End day here	**19.9 miles**
		St Bartholomew		
Wed	Briercliffe	St James	Start day here	2.5 miles
	Burnley	St Peters		6.4 miles
	Accrington	St John's		
	Baxenden	Christ the King	End day here	1.9 miles
		St John's		**10.8 miles**
Thur	Blackburn	The Redeemer Christ the King	Start day here	3.0 miles
	Darwen	St Cuthbert		
		St Peter		
	Standish	St Wilfred		6.7 miles
	Chorley	St Peter		2.7 miles
		St George		
		St Laurence		
	Whittle-le-Woods	St John	End day here	**12.4 miles**
Fri	Leyland	St John	Start day here	3.9 miles
	Farrington Moss	St Paul		2.1 miles
	Penwortham	St Leonard		3.0 miles
	Preston	St John & St George		6.8 miles
	Freckleton	Holy Trinity	End day here	**15.8 miles**
Sat	Lytham	St Cuthbert	Start day here	2.4 miles
	St Anne's on Sea	St Thomas		0.9 miles
	Heyhouses on Sea	St Anne		3.0 miles
	Squires Gate	St Mary's		1.2 miles
	South Shore	Holy Trinity	End day here	**6.6 miles**
Sun	Blackpool	Christ Church with All Saints	Start day here	3.5 miles
	Bispham	All Hallows		5.6 miles
	Fleetwood	St David	End of Walking	**9.1 miles**
		St Peter		
	Blackburn	Cathedral for Evensong – 4pm	Travel by Minibus – 31 miles	

ABOUT THE AUTHOR

Reverend Canon Dr Herrick Daniel had a great ambition to study medicine in his early life, but all this changed when he had a dramatic conversion at a Billy Graham's crusade in 1966. Having been called to the Church of England ministry, he was trained at Brasted and Trinity Theological Colleges. He is the holder of three degrees, including a postgraduate Certificate in Education.

Ordained at St. Paul's cathedral in London in 1975, he served two curacies at St Mark's, London and St Andrew's, Livesey, and priest in charge and vicar of St Barnabas, Blackburn, where he served successfully for twenty-seven years. He was made a canon in Blackburn Cathedral in 1998, and is well known in the diocese for converting an old co-op supermarket into a vibrant church, Christian bookshop and community centre. He is the founder and principal of St Barnabas Christian Foundation College, which was officially opened in 2001.

The author can be contacted at:
herrickdaniel@hotmail.co.uk

We hope you enjoyed reading this
Sovereign World book.
For more details of other Sovereign
books and new releases see our website:

www.sovereignworld.com

You can also join us on Facebook and Twitter.

To help us promote this title kindly consider
sharing your review in any of the following ways:
Via the Sovereign World Facebook page,
your blog, website or newsletter,
or at an online retailer review section.

_____

If you would like to help us send a copy of
this book and many other titles to needy
pastors in developing countries, please
write for further information or send
your gift to:

Sovereign World Trust
PO Box 777
Tonbridge,
Kent
TN11 0ZS
United Kingdom

www.sovereignworldtrust.org.uk

The Sovereign World Trust
is a registered charity.